Art and Lecture Out

Human Development
A Life-Span View

FIFTH EDITION

Robert V. Kail
Purdue University

John C. Cavanaugh
Pennsylvania State System of Higher Education

Prepared by

Ed Morris
Owensboro Community & Technical College

CENGAGE Learning

Australia • Brazil • Japan • Korea • Mexico • Singapore • Spain • United Kingdom • United States

CENGAGE Learning

For product information and technology assistance, contact us at **Cengage Learning Customer & Sales Support, 1-800-354-9706**

For permission to use material from this text or product, submit all requests online at **www.cengage.com/permissions**
Further permissions questions can be emailed to **permissionrequest@cengage.com**

ISBN-13: 978-0-495-59962-3
ISBN-10: 0-495-59962-X

Wadsworth
10 Davis Drive
Belmont, CA 94002-3098
USA

Cengage Learning is a leading provider of customized learning solutions with office locations around the globe, including Singapore, the United Kingdom, Australia, Mexico, Brazil, and Japan. Locate your local office at: **www.cengage.com/international**

Cengage Learning products are represented in Canada by Nelson Education, Ltd.

To learn more about Cengage Learning, visit **www.cengage.com/psychology**

Purchase any of our products at your local college store or at our preferred online store **www.ichapters.com**

Printed in the United States of America
1 2 3 4 5 6 7 12 11 10 09 08

TABLE OF CONTENTS

Chapter One
The Study of Human Development

1.1 Thinking About Development

Learning Objectives

- What fundamental issues of development have scholars addressed throughout history?
- What are the basic forces in the biopsychosocial framework?
- How does the timing of these forces make a difference in their impact?
- Recurring Issues in Human Development
- Nature Versus Nurture
- Continuity Versus Discontinuity
- Universal Versus Context-Specific Development

Basic Forces in Human Development: The Biopsychosocial Framework

- Biological Forces
- Psychological Forces
- Sociocultural Forces
- Life-Cycle Forces

1.2 Developmental Theories

Learning Objectives

- What is a developmental theory?
- How do psychodynamic theories account for development?
- What is the focus of learning theories of development?
- How do cognitive-developmental theories explain changes in thinking?
- What are the main points in the ecological and systems approach?
- What are the major tenets of life-span and life-cycle theories?

What is a Theory?

- "An organized set of ideas that is designed to explain development"
- Essential for developing predictions about behavior
- Predictions result in research that helps to support or clarify the theory

Major Theoretical Perspectives on Human Development

- Psychodynamic
  - Freud, Erikson
- Learning
  - Watson, Skinner, Bandura
- Cognitive
  - Piaget, Kohlberg

Chapter One

Psychodynamic: Erikson's Psychosocial Theory

- Basic Trust vs. Mistrust (0-1 year old)
- Autonomy vs. Shame and Doubt (1-3 years old)
- Initiative vs. Guilt (3-6 years old)
- Industry vs. Inferiority (6-Adolescence)
- Learning Theory
- Concentrates on how learning influences behavior
- Emphasizes the role of experience
- Stresses the influence of consequences on behavior
- Recognizes that people learn from watching others

Watson's Behaviorism

- Learning determines our behavior
- Experience is sufficient to explain the course of development
- Watson did little research to support his claims

B.F. Skinner's Operant Conditioning

- The consequences of a behavior determine whether it will be repeated
  - A reinforcement increases the chance that a behavior will be repeated
  - A punishment decreases the chance that a behavior will be repeated

Social Learning Theory

- Observational Learning, or Imitation
  - People learn by watching others
  - Imitation is more likely when the subject of observation is seen as smart, popular, or talented
  - Imitation is more likely when the subject of observation is rewarded for the behavior
  - Albert Bandura's Social Cognitive Theory
- Cognition emphasizes thinking
- We think about our experiences, trying to understand them
- Emphasizes how we perceive our world and our experiences
- Our perception influences our sense of self-efficacy, or our belief about our own abilities and talents

Cognitive-Developmental Theory

- Emphasizes the development of the thought processes as we mature
- Two approaches to the development of cognition:
  - We develop our thinking in stages (Piaget, Kohlberg)
  - Like computers, we become more efficient at processing information as we mature (Information-Processing Theory)

Chapter One

Jean Piaget's Cognitive Development Theory

- Children gradually learn more about how the world works by little "experiments" in which they test their understanding
- Cognitive development consists of stages in which children's understanding of their surroundings becomes increasingly complex and accurate
- Sensorimotor Stage (Birth to 2 years)
  - The Child interacts with the world through sensation and movement
  - Develops the ability to hold a mental representation of objects
- Preoperational Stage (2 to 7 years)
  - Develops the ability to use symbols
  - Egocentric: understands the world only from his/her own perspective
- Concrete Operational Thought (7 years to early adolescence)
  - Can use logic and reasoning
  - Cannot accurately consider the hypothetical
- Formal Operational Thought (Adolescence and beyond)
  - Thinks abstractly
  - Deals with the hypothetical concepts

Information-Processing Theory

- Uses the computer as a model of how thinking develops
- Mental Hardware: psychological structures such as memory capacity
- Mental Software: cognitive abilities that process information and help us to interact with the world

Vygotsky's Theory

- Emphasized the impact of sociocultural influence on child development
- Focused on how adults convey aspects of their culture to children
- Viewed development as an "apprenticeship"

The Ecological and Systems Approach

- Views all aspects of human development as interconnected
- No aspect of development alone can adequately explain development
- Understanding requires considering all factors: environmental, family, political, social, etc., and how they interact

Chapter One

Urie Bronfenbrenner's Theory: An Ecological Approach

- The Microsystem
  - People and objects in the immediate environment
- The Mesosystem
  - Influences of Microsystems on each other
- The Exosystem
  - Social, environmental, and governmental forces
- The Macrosystem
  - Subcultures and cultures in which the other systems are imbedded

Lawton & Nahemow's Competence-Environmental Press Theory

- Adaptation, or development, depends upon:
  - A person's abilities or "competencies"
  - Their environment and the demands it places on them
  - Emphasis is on how these factors interact

Questions Traditional Theories of Human Development Do Not Adequately Address

- Does development continue throughout the lifespan?
- What are the unique or specific developmental influences or issues of adulthood?
- How do we explain the apparent decline of abilities in later adulthood?

Current Perspectives

- Life-Span Perspective
  - There are many factors and one does not adequately explain development. All must be considered
- Selective Optimization with Compensation
  - Describes choices that determine and regulate development and aging
- The Life-Course Perspective
  - Examines how different generations experience and adjust to biological, psychological, and sociocultural forces within the historical time-period of their lives

Matilda Riley's Life-Span Perspective

- Emphasizes the need to view the entire life-span to understand a person's development
- The social, environmental, and historical aspects of one's life must be considered
- Learning about patterns of development influences society

Chapter One

Four Features of the Life-span Approach

- Multidirectionality
  - Different areas of development grow and decline at the same time
- Plasticity
  - Skills and abilities can be improved or developed throughout the life-span
- Historical Context
  - Historical time periods must be considered in examining development
- Multiple Causation
  - Biological, psychological, sociocultural, and life-cycle changes must be considered

Selective Optimization With Compensation (SOC)

- Elective Selection
  - Making choices to reduce involvement in order to concentrate on another
- Loss-based Selection
  - Reducing involvement because of lack of resources or abilities
- Compensation
  - Finding alternate ways of meeting goals due to loss of ability or diminished skills

The Life Course Perspective

- Emphasizes
  - How personal life-events interact with historical influences
  - How individual issues integrate with family issues
  - How earlier life events and the period of history in which they occurred shaped subsequent events and issues

The Big Picture

- Jim was a 25 year-old firefighter in Cincinnati. On September 11, 2001 he watched on television as the World Trade Center collapsed. He was so moved by the need to help his fellow firefighters, he went to New York to assist in the rescue efforts. Jim now suffers from Post Traumatic Stress Disorder after the weeks of intense work and emotion he experienced.
- How did Jim's age, his profession, and his choices interact to bring him to where he is today?
- What impact might this have on his work, family, and his health?
- How may these forces impact Jim's future job choices, his marriage, and feelings about political and racial issues?

1.3 Doing Developmental Research

Learning Objectives

- How do scientists measure topics of interest in studying human development?
- What research designs are used to study human development?
- How do researcher integrate results from multiple studies?
- What ethical procedures must researchers follow?
- How do investigators communicate results from research studies?
- How does research affect public policy?

Measurement in Human Development Research

- Systematic Observation
  - Naturalistic Observation
- "Real-life" observations
  - Structured Observation
- Researcher creates a situation likely to result in a type of behavior in which she/he is interested

Other Behavioral Measures

- Sampling Behavior with Tasks
- Self Reports
- Physiological Measures

Evaluating Research Methods

- Reliability
  - Does this method consistently measure what is being studied?
- Validity
  - Does this measure provide a true picture of what is being studied?

Representational Sampling

- Populations
  - Broad groups of people in which researchers may be interested
- Sample
  - A subset of the population chosen to represent the population

General Research Designs

- Correlational Studies
  - Measures relationship between variables as they are observed naturally in the world
  - Provides an index called the correlation coefficient ("r") which indicates the strength of the relationship between variables
  - Correlation does not prove causation

Chapter One

Experimental Studies

- Studies the effect of one variable on another
  Studies possible "cause and effect" relationship
  - The Independent Variable is the factor that is being manipulated
  - The Dependent Variable is the behavior that is studied for possible change

Designs For Studying Development

- Longitudinal Studies
  - Observes or tests one group of individuals over a long period
    - Is expensive and requires a large time commitment
- Cross-Sectional Studies
  - Observes or tests groups of different ages
    - More time-effective, less expensive, but cannot show small changes of continuity of development
- Sequential Studies
- A combination of cross-sectional and longitudinal designs
- Allows for flexibility to collect information in several ways
- Avoids cohort effects

Integrating Findings From Different Studies

- Meta-analysis
  - Analysis of many studies to estimate relations between variables
  - Allows scientists to verify findings across many studies

Conducting Research Ethically

- Minimize and warn of any risks to participants
- "Informed Consent"
- Avoid deception
- Individual results or data must be kept anonymous or confidential

Communicating Research Results

- Research results are published in scientific journals
- To be published in journals, research results must be useful, well-done, and original

Applying Research Results: Social Policy

- Think About This:
- How does being a participant in a scientific study affect behavior?
- What if the only way to collect valid information about a factor requires putting subjects at risk, or not informing them of possible risks?

Chapter Two
Biological Foundations: Heredity, Prenatal Development, and Birth

2.1 In the Beginning

Learning Objectives

- What are chromosomes and genes? How do they carry hereditary information from one generation to the next?
- What are common problems involving chromosomes and what are their consequences?
- How is a child's heredity influenced by the environment in which they grow up?

In The Beginning

- Mechanisms of Heredity
- Human eggs contain 23 chromosomes selected from the mother's 46. One chromosome is selected from each of the 23 pairs of chromosomes
- Human sperm contain 23 chromosomes selected from the father's 46. One chromosome is selected from each of the 23 pairs
- The human egg and sperm unite, resulting in a zygote which contains a complete set of 46 chromosomes
- The first 22 pairs of chromosomes are called autosomes
- The 23rd pair determines the gender of the child and is called the sex chromosomes
- The 46 chromosomes contain around 30,000 genes

Mechanisms of Heredity

- The 23rd Pair of Chromosomes
  - Males carry XY chromosomes - X from mother and Y from father
  - Females carry XX chromosomes - X from mother and X from father
- The complete set of inherited traits are called a genotype
- How the traits are expressed is called phenotype and is the combined effects of genotype and environmental influences

Alleles

- Characteristics are determined by the interaction of genes on the two chromosomes in a pair
- Each chromosome of a pair contains one parent's contribution to a specific trait
- When the genes are the same they are called homozygous; when different, they are called heterozygous
- Homozygous Alleles
  - When alleles are the same, both parents have contributed similar genes for a trait
- Heterozygous Alleles
  - The parents have contributed different versions of the trait

Chapter Two

Genetic Disorders

- Inherited Disorders involve dominant or recessive alleles for conditions such as Sickle-Cell Disease, PKU, and Huntington's Disease
- Extra, missing, or damaged chromosomes result in abnormalities of development (e.g., Down Syndrome, Turner's Syndrome, and Klinefelter's Syndrome)

Heredity, Environment, and Development

- Behavioral Genetics
  - The study of the inheritance of behavioral and psychological traits

Polygenetic Inheritance

- When many genes affect the phenotype of a trait
- Many psychological and behavioral characteristics are polygenetic and are impossible to trace to a single gene

Twins

- Dizygotic (fraternal) twins come from two different eggs fertilized by two different sperm
- Monozygotic (identical) twins come from the union of one egg and one sperm that splits in two soon after conception

What Twin Studies Can Teach Us

- Fraternal twins, while they share much of the same experience and environment, have no more genetic similarity than other siblings
- Identical twins share much of the same experience but are also genetically identical

Paths From Genes to Behavior

- Genes' impact on behavior depend on the environment
  - Reaction range
- Heredity and environment interact throughout development
- Genes can influence the kind of environment to which a person is exposed
- Environmental influences typically make children within a family different

Chapter Two

2.2 From Conception to Birth
Learning Objectives

Periods of Prenatal Development
- Period of the Zygote (Weeks 1-2)
  - After fertilization, the zygote travels down the fallopian tube and is implanted in the uterine wall
- Period of the Embryo (Weeks 3-8)
  - Body structures, internal organs, and the three layers of the embryo (ectoderm, mesoderm, & endoderm) develop
  - The amniotic sac fills with fluid and the umbilical cord connects the embryo to the placenta
- Period of the Fetus (Week 9-Birth)
  - Week 9- Differentiation of the ovaries and testes
  - Week 12- Circulatory system begins to function
  - Week 16- Movement felt by mother
  - Week 32- Age of viability

Conception in the 21st Century
- *In vitro* fertilization
- Inserting sperm directly into the Fallopian tubes
- Injecting sperm directly into the egg

Principles of Growth
- Cephalocaudal Principle
  - Growth from head to spine
- Proximodistal Principle
  - Growth from areas close to the body to farthest from body

2.3 Influences on Prenatal Development
Learning Objectives
- How is prenatal development influenced by a pregnant woman's age, her nutrition, and the stress she experiences while pregnant?
- How do diseases, drugs, and environmental hazards sometimes affect prenatal development?
- What general principles affect the ways that prenatal development can be harmed?
- How can prenatal development be monitored? Can abnormal prenatal development be corrected?

General Risk Factors

- Nutrition
  - Inadequate maternal nutrition may result in premature birth and low birth weight
  - Lack of folic acid may increase risk of *spina bifida*
- Stress
  - Studies show extreme maternal stress is associated with low birth weight and premature births
- Mother's Age
  - Older mothers are more likely to have difficulty getting pregnant, miscarriages, and stillbirths
  - Nearly 50% of pregnancies among women in their 40s and 50s result in miscarriage

Teratogens: Drugs

- Known harmful agents include:
  - Alcohol, aspirin, caffeine, nicotine
- Fetal Alcohol Syndrome
  - Results from overuse of alcohol during pregnancy
  - Children with FAS may have mental retardation, facial deformities, and heart defects

Teratogens: Diseases

- AIDS, Cytomegalovirus, Genital Herpes, Rubella (German Measles), Syphilis
- Effects include:
  - neurological disorders
  - deafness
  - blindness
  - mental disability
  - damage to bones, eyes, ears, or heart

Teratogens: Environmental Hazards

- Lead, Mercury, PCBs, X-Rays
- Effects may include:
  - mental disability
  - retarded growth
  - cerebral palsy
  - impaired memory and verbal skill
  - retarded growth
  - leukemia

Chapter Two

How Teratogens Influence Prenatal Development

- The effect of the teratogen depends upon the genotype of the organism
- The impact of teratogens changes over the course of prenatal development
- Each teratogen affects a specific aspect of prenatal development
- The impact of teratogens depends on the dosage
- Damage from teratogens is not always evident at birth

Diagnosis and Treatment

- Genetic Counseling
  - Helps to assess the chances of inherited disorders
- Prenatal Diagnosis
  - Ultrasound
  - Amniocentesis
  - Chorionic Villus Sampling

Prenatal Diagnosis and Treatment

- Fetal Medicine
  - Administering medicine to the fetus
  - Fetal surgery to correct spina bifida and circulatory problems
  - Genetic engineering involves replacing defective genes with synthetic normal genes

2.4 Labor and Delivery

Learning Objectives

- What are the different phases of labor and delivery?
- What are "natural" ways of coping with the pain of childbirth? Is childbirth at home safe?
- What adjustments do parents face after a baby's birth?
- What are some complications that can occur during birth?
- What contributes to infant mortality in the developed and least developed countries?

Stages of Labor

- Stage 1 lasts 12-24 hours for the first birth and includes contractions and the enlargement of the cervix to approximately 10 centimeters
- Stage 2 includes the actual birth of the baby and lasts about an hour
- Stage 3 lasts a few minutes and involves expelling of the placenta

Approaches to Childbirth

- Childbirth Classes
  - Explains what happens during pregnancy and delivery
  - Teaches techniques to manage the pain of childbirth. The emphasis is on natural methods, relaxation, and coaching
  - Studies show that mothers who attend childbirth classes typically use less medication

Chapter Two

Birthing Alternatives

- Home Births
  - Less Expensive
  - Parents have more control over the conditions
  - Birth problems are no more common at home than at the hospital when pregnancy has been problem-free
- Birthing Centers
  - More home-like than hospitals, but in a clinic setting independent of hospitals

Labor and Delivery: Birth Complications

- Hypoxia, or inadequate blood and oxygen to baby
- Complications may result in cesarean section (C-section)
- Births before the 36th week are called premature or preterm
- Babies weighing less than 5.5 pounds have low birth weight
- Babies weighing less than 3.3 pounds have very low birth weight
- Below 2.2 pounds is called extremely low birth weight

Infant Mortality

- Infant Mortality is the number of infants out of 1,000 births that die before the age of 1 year
- U.S. mortality rate is just under 1%, or 7 of 1000
- 15 industrialized nations have lower infant mortality than U.S
- Possible factors include low birth weight resulting from a lack of free or inexpensive prenatal care and fewer paid leave of absences for pregnant women

Chapter Three
The Newborn

3.1 The Newborn

Learning Objectives

- How do reflexes help newborns interact with the world?
- How do we determine whether a baby is healthy and adjusting to life outside the uterus?
- What behavioral states are common among newborns?
- What are the different features of temperament? Do they change as children grow?

The Newborn's Reflexes

- The newborn is born with certain specific responses that are triggered by specific stimuli
- Some of these reflexes, such as rooting and sucking, appear to have survival implications
- Other reflexes appear to be precursors for later voluntary motor behavior
- The newborn's reflexes may also reflect the health of the child's nervous system

Assessing the Newborn

- The Apgar Index
  - Heart rate
  - Respiration
  - Muscle tone
  - Reflexes
  - Skin tone
- Neonatal Behavioral Assessment Scale (NBAS)
  - Includes 28 behavioral items
  - Assesses infant's autonomic, motor, and social systems

The Newborn's States

- Alert Inactivity
- Waking Activity
- Crying
- Sleeping

Crying

- Basic Cry
  - Starts softly and builds in volume and intensity.
  - Often seen when the child is hungry
- Mad Cry
  - More intense and louder
- Pain Cry
  - Starts with a loud wail, followed by a long pause, then gasping

Sleeping
- Newborns sleep an average of 16-18 hours daily
- Newborns usually follow a sleep-wake cycle of around 4 hours of sleep followed by 1 hour of wakefulness
- By 3 or 4 months newborns usually sleep through the night
- REM sleep gradually decreases from 50% of the newborn's sleep to about 25% at the age of 1 year

Co-sleeping
- The practice of sleeping in the same room or bed with the child
- Research shows no evidence of increased dependence
- Co-sleeping has the advantage of avoiding elaborate sleep-time rituals

Sudden Infant Death Syndrome (SIDS)
- SIDS is the sudden, unexplainable death of a healthy baby
- The exact causes of SIDS are unknown. May be related to parent's smoking, the child sleeping on their stomach, and overheating
- Risk is reduced when infants sleep on their back
- African American infants are twice as likely to die from SIDS because they are more likely to be placed on their stomachs to sleep

Dimensions of Temperament
- Activity Level
  - Motor activity
- Positive Affect
  - Pleasure, enthusiasm, and contentment
- Persistence
  - Amount of resistance to distraction
- Inhibition
  - Extent of shyness and withdrawal
- Negative Affect
  - Irritability and tendency toward anger

Rothbart & Hwang: Theory of Temperament
- Surgency/extraversion
  - How happy, active, and stimulation-seeking is the child?
- Negative affect
  - Is the child angry, fearful, frustrated, shy and not easily soothed?
- Effortful control
  - Can the child focus their attention and inhibit responses?

Chapter Three

Hereditary and Environmental Contributions to Temperament

- Twin Studies
  - The correlation of activity levels in fraternal twins was found to be .38
  - For identical twins the correlation in activity levels was found to be .72
  - Similar findings for social fearfulness, persistence, and proneness to anger

Stability of Temperament

- Studies suggest that temperament tends to be somewhat stable throughout infancy and the toddler years

3.2 Physical Development
Learning Objectives

- How do height and weight change from birth to 2 years of age?
- What nutrients do young children need? How are they best provided?
- What are the consequences of malnutrition? How can it be treated?
- What are nerve cells, and how are they organized in the brain?
- How does the brain develop? When does it begin to function?

Growth of the Body

- Growth is more rapid in infancy than during any other period after birth
- Infants double their weight by three months
- Infants triple their weight by 1 year
- Average is not the same as Normal

Nutrition and Growth

- Because growth is so rapid, young babies must consume large amounts of calories relative to body weight
- Breast-feeding is the best way to ensure proper nourishment
- New foods should be introduced one at a time

Malnutrition

- World-wide about 1 in 4 children under 5 are malnourished (UNICEF, 2006)
- Malnourished children develop more slowly
- Malnutrition is most damaging during infancy due to rapid growth rate

The Emerging Nervous System

- The brain and the rest of the nervous system consists of cells known as neurons
- Neurons consist of a soma, dendrites, the axon, and terminal buttons
- Terminal buttons release chemicals called neurotransmitters

Chapter Three

The Brain
- The brain has 50-100 billion neurons
- The wrinkled surface of the brain is called the cortex
- The two halves of the brain are called hemispheres
- The two hemispheres are connected by the corpus callosum

The Making of the Working Brain
- The brain weighs about three-quarters of a pound at birth – about 25% of an adult brain
- At around 3 years of age the child's brain is about 80% of an adult's brain weight

Emerging Brain Structures
- At 3 weeks after conception the neural plate, a flat structure of cells, forms
- By 28 weeks after conception, the brain has all the neurons it will ever have
- In the 4th month of prenatal development, axons begin to form myelin, which helps to speed transmission

Structure and Function: Brain-Mapping Methods
- Studies of children with brain damage
- Electroencephalogram (EEG) studies of infants
- Functional Magnetic Resonance Imaging (F-MRI) tracks blood flow in the brain

Brain Plasticity
- Neuroplasticity: The brain shows flexibility in the development of its organization
- While individuals' brains show similar structure and function, environmental demands may affect organization and mapping of the brain

Neuroplasticity
- Experience-expectant growth
  - The development of the brain is affected by experiences that are common to most humans
- Experience-dependent growth
  - Changes in the brain that are not linked to specific points in development and vary across individuals and cultures

3.3 Early Motor Skills
Learning Objectives
- What are the component skills involved in learning to walk? At what age do infants master them?
- How do infants learn to coordinate the use of their hands?

Locomotion
- By 7 months, infants can sit alone
- At around 14 months toddlers may stand alone
- Dynamic Systems Theory
  - The idea that motor development involves many distinct skills that are organized and reorganized over time to meet demands of specific tasks

Chapter Three

Posture and Balance

- Infants are "top-heavy" and easily lose their balance
- Within a few months, infants use inner ear and visual cues to adjust posture
- Infants must relearn balance each time they achieve new postures

Stepping

- Many infants move their legs in a stepping-like motion as early as 6-7 months
- Walking unassisted is not possible until other skills are mastered and the child is developmentally ready

Coordinating Skills

- Walking skills must be learned separately and then integrated with others
- Differentiation: Mastery of component skills
- Integration: Combining them in sequence to accomplish the task

Cultural Impact on Motor Development

- Some cultural practices encourage certain early motor skills
- Various cultures have different practices that may discourage early motor development
- Despite cultural differences in average age of skill development, children acquire skills within a normal range

Fine Motor Skills

- At 4 months, infants clumsily reach for objects
- By 5 months, infants coordinate movement of the two hands
- By 2-3 years, children can use zippers but not buttons
- Tying shoes is a skill that develops around age 6 years

Handedness

- About 90% of children prefer to use their right hand
- Most children grasp with their right hand by age 13 months and a clear preference is seen by 2 years
- Preference is affected by heredity but environmental factors influence it too

3.4 Perception

Learning Objectives

- Are infants able to smell, to taste, and to experience pain?
- Can infants hear? How do they use sound to locate objects?
- How well can infants see? Can they see color and depth?
- How do infants coordinate information between different sensory modalities, such as between vision and hearing?

Chapter Three

Coming to Know the World: Perception

- Newborns have a good sense of smell
  - They react to pleasant and unpleasant
  - They turn toward pads soaked in their own amniotic fluid, or the odors of their mother's breast
- Newborns can differentiate between tastes
  - They differentiate between salty, sour, bitter, and sweet
  - Facial reactions are obvious reactions to sweet tastes

Touch and Pain

- Babies react to touch with reflexes and other movements
- Babies react to painful stimuli with the pain cry – a sudden, high-pitched wail – and they are not easily soothed

Hearing

- Startle reactions suggest that infants are sensitive to sound
- 6-month-olds distinguish between different pitches as well as adults
- By 7 months, infants can use sound to locate direction and distance

Seeing

- Newborns respond to light and track moving objects with their eyes
- Visual Acuity (clarity of vision) is the smallest pattern that can be distinguished dependably
- Infants at 1 month see at 20 feet what adults see at 200-400 feet
- By 1 year, the infant's visual acuity is the same as adults

Color

- Newborns perceive few colors
- 1-month-old infants can differentiate between blue and gray, as well as red from green
- 3- to 4-month-old infants can perceive colors similarly to adults

Depth

- Visual cliff studies show that children as young as 6 weeks react with emotional indicators or interest to differences in depth
- At 7 months, they show fear of the deep side of the cliff
- Infants at 4-6 months use retinal disparity (the difference between the images of objects in each eye) to discern depth
- Infants of 5 months use motion and interposition to perceive depth

Chapter Three

Depth Perception
- Children use cues to infer depth, including:
  - Kinetic Cues
  - Visual Expansion
  - Motion Parallax
  - Retinal Disparity
- By 7 months, children use Pictorial Cues such as:
  - Linear Perspective
  - Texture Gradient

Perceiving Objects
- Perception of objects is limited in newborns, but develops soon
- Infants group objects together that have the same texture, color, or aligned edges

Perceiving Faces
- Newborns prefer to look at moving faces until around 4 weeks, then track all moving objects
- At first, infants process faces as though they are unrelated elements within a collection
- By 7-8 months, infants process faces similarly to adults, as a unique arrangement of features

Integrating Sensory Information
- Infants soon begin to perceive the link between visual images and sounds
- Infants seem to pay more attention to intersensory redundancy, or information simultaneously coming from different sensory modes

3.5 Becoming Self-Aware
Learning Objectives
- When do children begin to realize that they exist?
- What are toddlers' and preschoolers' self-concepts like?
- When do preschool children begin to acquire a theory of mind?

Origins of Self Concept
- 9-month-old infants smile at the face in the mirror but do not seem to recognize it as their own face
- By 15-24 months, infants see the image in the mirror and touch their own face, suggesting that they know that the image in the mirror is theirs
- Preschoolers can describe their physical characteristics, preferences, and competencies

Theory of Mind
- By age 2, children understand that people have desires and these cause behavior
- 3-year-olds can distinguish between the mental world and the physical world
- 4-year-olds understand that behavior is based on beliefs and that the beliefs can be wrong

Chapter Four
The Emergence of Thought and Language: Cognitive Development in Infancy and Early Childhood

4.1 Piaget's Account

Learning Objectives

- According to Piaget, how do schemes, assimilation, and accommodation provide the foundation for cognitive development throughout the life span?
- How does thinking become more advanced as infants progress through the sensorimotor stage?
- What are the distinguishing characteristics of thinking during the preoperational stage?
- What are the strengths and weaknesses of Piaget's theory?
- How have contemporary researchers extended Piaget's theory?

Basic Principles of Cognitive Development

- Children make sense of the world through schemes
- Children adapt to their environment as they develop by adding and refining their schemes
- Schemes change from physical, to functional, conceptual, and abstract as the child develops

Piaget's Account: Assimilation and Accommodation

- When new experiences fit into existing
- schemes it is called assimilation
- When schemes have to be modified as a consequence of new experiences, it is called accommodation
- Assimilation is required to benefit from experience. Accommodation allows for dealing with completely new data or experiences

Piaget's Account: Equilibration

- Equilibrium - balance between assimilation and accommodation
- Disequilibrium - more accommodation than assimilation
- Equilibration - inadequate schemes are replaced with more advanced and mature schemes
- Equilibration occurs three times during development, resulting in 4 stages of cognitive development

Piaget's Account: Periods of Cognitive Development

- Sensorimotor Period (0-2 years)
- Infancy
- Preoperational Period (2-7 years)
- Preschool and early elementary school
- Concrete Operational Period (7-11 years)
- Middle and late elementary school
- Formal Operational Period (11 years & up)
- Adolescence and adulthood

Piaget's Account: Sensorimotor Thinking

- Object permanence
- Using symbols

Chapter Four

Piaget's Account: Preoperational Thinking

- Egocentrism
- Animism
- Centration
- Conservation
- Appearance is Reality

Criticisms of Piaget's Theory

- Piaget underestimates cognitive ability in infants and overestimates in adolescents
- Piaget is vague about mechanisms and processes of change
- He does not account for variability in children's performance
- His theory undervalues the influence of sociocultural environment

Extending Piaget's Account: Children's Naive Theories

- Naive Physics
- Studies that investigate the age at which children learn there is conflict between current understanding and the true nature of objects
- Naive Biology
- 4-year-olds know that living things move, grow, and heal themselves
- Know that inanimate objects have to be moved, do not grow, and have to be fixed

4.2 Information Processing

Learning Objectives

- What is the basis of the information-processing approach?
- How well do young children pay attention?
- What kinds of learning take place during infancy?
- Do infants and preschool children remember?
- What do infants and preschooler know about numbers?

Information Processing: General Principles

- Human thinking is understood along a computer model
- Mental Hardware are neural and mental structures that enable the mind to operate
- Mental Software are mental programs that allow for the performance of specific tasks

Information Processing Processes: Attention

- When sensory information receives additional cognitive processing it is called attention
- Emotional and physical reactions to unfamiliar stimulus causes an orienting response
- A lessening of the reaction to a new stimulus is called habituation

Chapter Four

Information Processing Processes: Learning

- Classical Conditioning
- A neutral stimulus becomes able to elicit a response that was previously caused by another stimulus
- Operant Conditioning
- Behaviors are affected by their consequences
- Imitation
- Older children learn by observing others

Information Processing Processes: Memory

- Studies show that as early as 2-3 months children remember past events, forget them over time, and remember them again with cues
- During the preschool years, children develop autobiographical memory for significant events in their own past

Preschoolers on the Witness Stand

Information Processing Processes: Learning Number Skills

- Ordinality: Knowing that numbers can differ in size and being able to tell which is greater
- One-to-one principle: There is a number name for each object counted
- Stable-order principle: Number names must be counted in the same order
- Cardinality principle: The last number in a counting sequence denotes the number of objects

4.3 Mind & Culture: Vygotsky's Theory

Learning Objectives

- What is the zone of proximal development? How does it help explain how children accomplish more when they collaborate with others?
- Why is scaffolding a particularly effective way of teaching youngsters new concepts and skills?
- When and why do children talk to themselves as they solve problems?

Lev Vygotsky (1896-1934)

- A Russian psychologist
- Saw cognitive development as an apprenticeship in which children advance by interaction with others more mature
- Vygotsky died young (37) and did not fully develop his theory beyond childhood

Mind & Culture: Vygotsky's Theory Major Contributions

- Zone of Proximal Development
  - The difference between what children can do with and without help from a more experienced guide
  - Teachers should attempt to keep students in this zone in order to achieve maximum achievement

- Scaffolding
  - Giving just enough assistance
  - Studies show that students do not learn as well when told everything to do, nor when left alone to discover on their own

Private Speech

- Children talk to themselves as they go about difficult tasks
- This speech is not intended for others, but for self guidance and regulation
- Eventually this private speech becomes internalized and becomes inner speech… which was Vygotsky's term for thought

4.4 Language

Learning Objectives

- When do infants first hear and make speech sounds?
- When do children start to talk? How do they learn word meanings?
- How do young children learn grammar?
- How well do youngsters communicate?

Language: The Road to Speech

- Perceiving Speech
- Phonemes- The smallest sounds
- Studies show that as early as 1 month infants can distinguish between sounds
- Different languages use different sets of phonemes
- Children practice all phonemes, gradually restricting their use to only those phonemes to which they are exposed
- Eventually, they lose the ability to distinguish unused phonemes

Language: Identifying Words

- Children learn to pay more attention to often repeated and emphasized words
- Parents use infant-directed speech in which they speak slowly and exaggerate changes in pitch and volume
- Sometimes called motherese because it was first observed in mothers

Language: Steps to Speech

- At 2 months, infants begin cooing
- Around 6 months, toddlers begin babbling
- At 8-11 months children incorporate intonation, or changes in pitch that are typical of the language they hear

Language: First Words & Many More

- Around 1 year, children use their first words, usually consonant-vowel pairs such as "dada" or "wawa"
- By 2 years, children have a vocabulary of around a few hundred words
- By age 6, children know around 10,000 words
- Some children use a referential style vocabulary to name objects, persons, or actions
- Other children use an expressive style to make statements resembling single words

Chapter Four

Language: Fast Mapping of Words

- Connecting new words to that which they refer helps to infer the meaning of the new word
- Parents pay attention to what children are attracted to and provide guidance, which is called joint attention
- Children seem to understand constraints on word names that help to infer meaning
- Types of constraints on word names include:
- If an unfamiliar word is heard in the presence of objects that already have names and objects that don't, the word must refer to one of the objects that doesn't have a name
- Names refer to the whole object and not just a part of it
- Children use sentence cues to infer the meaning of unfamiliar words
- Cognitive factors, such as better attentional and perceptual skills, assist in learning language
- Naming errors result from underextension (defining words too narrowly) and overextension (defining words too broadly)

Language: Individual Differences in Word Learning

- Vocabulary ranges from 25 to 250 words at 18 months
- Phonological Memory - The ability to remember speech sounds briefly
- Referential Style - Mainly naming of objects, persons, or actions
- Expressive Style - Includes social phrases

Word Learning Styles Language: Encouraging Language Growth

- Parents assist in learning language by:
- Speaking to children frequently
- Naming objects of children's attention
- Using speech that is more grammatically sophisticated
- Reading to them
- Encouraging watching television programs with an emphasis on learning new words, such as Sesame Street

Language: Speaking in Sentences

- Two- and three-word sentences, called telegraphic speech, begin around 18 months
- Children may leave out grammatical morphemes, or words and endings that make a sentence correct
- The application of rules to words that are exceptions to the rules is called overregularization

How do Children Acquire Grammar?

- The Behaviorist answer
  - Imitation and reinforcement
- The Linguistic answer
  - Innate mechanisms that simplify the task of learning grammar
- The Cognitive answer
  - Look for patterns, detect irregularities, create rules
- The Social-Interactive answer
  - Eclectic use of all of the explanations to describe language development

Language: Communicating With Others

- Effective communication requires:
- Taking turns as speaker and listener
- Making sure to speak in language the listener understands
- Paying attention while listening and making sure the speaker knows if he/she is being understood

Chapter Five
Entering the Social World: Socioemotional Development in Infancy and Early Childhood

5.1 Beginnings: Trust & Attachment

Learning Objectives

- What are Erikson's first three stages of psychosocial development?
- How do infants form emotional attachments to mother, father, and other significant people in their lives?
- What are the different varieties of attachment relationships, how do they arise, and what are their consequences?
- Is attachment jeopardized when parents of infants and young children are employed outside of the home?

Erikson's Stages of Early Psychosocial Development

- Basic Trust vs. Mistrust (Infancy)
  - Infants are dependent on caregivers to meet their needs and provide comfort
  - The responsiveness and consistency with which caregivers meet these needs helps to develop a basic sense of trust and openness in the child
  - If these needs are not met, the child develops wariness and a lack of comfort
- Autonomy vs. Shame and Doubt (1-3 years)
  - Children develop a sense of control over their own actions
  - If autonomy is not achieved, children are shameful and doubt their own capabilities
- Initiative vs. Guilt (3-5 years)
  - Children develop imagination for possibilities for themselves
  - Play becomes purposeful and includes paying the roles of mother, father, teacher, or athlete
  - With proper encouragement and balance, initiative and cooperation are developed

The Growth of Attachment

- Evolutionary Psychology views many human behaviors as successful adaptations to the environment
- Security in the presence of another, along with need for physical closeness is attachment
- Bowlby noticed that children who form attachments to an adult are more likely to survive
- Attachments are usually formed with the mother but may be any responsive and caring person

Steps Toward Attachment

- Preattachment stage (Birth to 6-8 weeks)
- Attachment in the making (6-8 weeks to 6-8 months)
- True Attachment (6-8 months to 18 months)
- Reciprocal Relationships (18 months on)

Father-Infant Relationships

- Attachment for fathers tends to follow that with mothers
- Fathers tend to spend more time playing with children than taking care of them
- Fathers play with children differently than mothers (more rough-and-tumble)
- Children tend to seek out the father for a playmate. Mothers are preferred for comfort

Forms of Attachment

- The strange situation experiment
  - Ainsworth introduced children and mothers to a room from which the mother then left. Upon her return, the nature of the child's reaction was studied
  - Four types of reactions were observed

The Four Reactions to the Strange Situation:

- Secure Attachment - on the mother's return, the child is comforted, crying stops, and the child begins to explore again
- Avoidant Attachment - on the mother's return the child ignores or turns away
- Resistant Attachment - the baby is upset and remains upset when mother returns and is difficult to console
- Disorganized Attachment - the child seems confused and is unsure of reaction
- Percentage of children in categories of reaction to the Strange Situation:
  - Secure Attachment: 60-65% of U.S. babies
  - Avoidant Attachment: 20% of U.S. babies
  - Resistant Attachment: 15% of U.S. babies
  - Disorganized Attachment: 5-10% of U.S. babies

Consequences of Attachment

- Children with secure attachments are more confident and successful with peers
- Securely attached children have fewer conflicts with friendships with peers
- The conclusion is that children use early attachments as prototypes for later relationships and interactions

Attachment, Work, & Alternate Caregiving

- NICHD research suggested:
  - No relationship between quality of the daycare and mother-child attachment
  - No relationship between length of stays or changes in daycare and parent attachment
  - Quality of attachment was found to be more related to the sensitivity of the mother to the child's needs and care

Chapter Five

Characteristics of High-Quality Daycare

- Low ratio of children to caregivers
- Well-trained and experienced staff
- Low staff turnover
- Ample educational and social stimulation
- Good communication between parents and daycare workers

5.2 Emerging Emotions

Learning Objectives

- At what ages do children begin to express basic emotions?
- What are complex emotions and when do they develop?
- When do children begin to understand other people's emotions? How do they use this information to guide their own behavior?

Experiencing and Expressing Emotions

- Joy, anger, and fear are considered basic emotions
- Basic emotions consist of:
  - A subjective feeling
  - A physiological change
  - An overt behavior

Measuring Emotions

- Facial expressions indicate emotional state
  - Infants all over the world express emotions similarly, suggesting biological programming
  - By 5-6 months, infants' facial expressions change in reaction to events
  - Close resemblance between adult and infant smiles suggest facial expressions have similar meaning

Development of Basic Emotions

- At 2-3 months, children begin smiling in response to human faces. These are called social smiles
- Around 6 months, children show stranger wariness in the presence of an unfamiliar adult

Emergence of Complex Emotions

- Complex emotions emerge around 18-24 months
- Complex emotions include:
  - Guilt
  - Embarrassment
  - Pride

Cultural Differences in Emotional Expression

- Many emotions are expressed similarly around the world
- Some differences have been observed
  - Asian children are encouraged to show emotional restraint
  - European American 11-month-olds cried and smiled more than Chinese infants of same age

Recognizing & Using Others' Emotions

- At 4-6 months, infants can distinguish facial expression and the emotions they portray
- Infants look to parents' face for cues to help interpret a situation in social referencing
- A positive and rewarding relationship with parents and siblings improves children's understanding of emotions

Regulating Emotions

- By 4-6 months, children can use simple strategies to regulate their emotions
- Older children and adolescents
  - Become less dependent upon others to control their emotions
  - Begin to use mental strategies to regulate emotions
  - Look for ways to regulate emotions that work. They adapt the method to the situation

5.3 Interacting With Others

Learning Objectives

- When do youngsters first begin to play with each other? How does play change during infancy and the preschool years?
- What determines whether children help one another?

The Joys of Play

- Around 1 year, children begin engaging in parallel play, or playing alongside each other without much interaction
- At 15-18 months, children do similar activities and smile at each other in simple social play
- At about 2 years, children engage in cooperative play. They play roles and interact

Make-Believe

- Play roles that reflect values and traditions
- Is entertaining and promotes cognitive development
- May help children to explore topics that frighten them
- Imaginary playmates promote imagination and sociability
- Pretend play is a regular part of preschooler's play but may be understood by 16-18 months

Solitary Play

- Usually not an indicator of problems
- Wandering aimlessly or hovering over others playing may be reason to seek professional consultation

Gender Differences in Play

- Between 2-3, children prefer to play with peers of their own gender
- Children resist playing with members of the opposite sex
- Children prefer like-sexed playmates for all types of activities
  - Girls tend to support girl peers in enabling
  - Boys tend to contradict, threaten, and compete with boy peers in activity known as constricting

Chapter Five

Parental Influence
- Parents tend to help in activities and pretend along with young children
- Parents may play mediator in settling disputes
- Parents may also play a coaching role in diffusing aggression and competition
- Children whose parents engage in these activities are often more socially skillful

Helping Others
- Prosocial behavior is any behavior that benefits others
- Altruism is behavior that does not benefit oneself but does benefit others, such as helping and sharing
- Children as young as 18 months are observed to engage in altruistic behaviors, such as comforting or hugging peers in pain

Skills Underlying Altruistic Behavior
- Being able to take the perspective of others is called empathy
- Empathy is more likely when a child reaches school age
- Children who empathize are more likely to help

Factors Influencing Children's Altruism
- Feelings of responsibility for the child in need
- Feelings of competence
  - Do they have the skills necessary to help?
- Mood: Children who are happy or feeling successful are more likely to help
- Costs of altruism
  - Will helping require sacrifice?

Socialization of Altruism
- Parents may foster altruism by:
  - Modeling
  - Disciplinary practices that include reasoning, warmth, and feedback
  - Providing opportunities to behave prosocially

5.4 Gender Roles & Gender Identity
Learning Objectives
- What are our stereotypes about males and females? How well do they correspond to actual differences between boys and girls?
- How do young children learn gender roles?
- How are gender roles changing? What further changes might the future hold?

Images of Men & Women: Facts & Fantasy
- Learning Gender Stereotypes
  - Belief and images about males and females that may or may not be true
  - 5-year-olds tend to believe that boys are strong and dominant and girls are emotional and gentle
  - After preschool, children achieve more flexibility in their beliefs about gender stereotypes

Chapter Five

Gender-related Differences

- Girls have larger vocabularies and read, write, and spell better. They also have fewer language problems
- Boys perform better on math achievement tests but girls get better grades in math courses
- Boys are more accurate and rapid in visual-spatial tasks
- Girls tend to be more compliant with the directions of adults. They also are more likely to be influenced by others
- Boys are more physically aggressive in situations in which they are provoked. Girls are higher in relational aggression, or hurting others by damaging their relationships with peers
- Girls are better able to express and interpret emotions

Gender Typing

- Parents tend to be equally warm and encouraging to boys and girls
- Parents tend to encourage playing with dolls and dressing up more with daughters than with sons. Rough and tumble play is tolerated more in boys
- Parents assign different household chores to boys and girls
- The difference in treatment between boys and girls tends to be greater for fathers
- Fathers punish their sons more, and are more accepting of dependence in girls
- Early like-sex play may also reflect peer influence of gender roles

Gender Identity

- By age 2-3 children identify themselves as either a boy or a girl
- By preschool age, children know that gender is stable, but may believe that boys who play with dolls will become a girl
- Between 4 and 7 years-of-age, children understand gender constancy – that gender does not change

Biological Inflences

- Studies of children with Congenital Adrenal hyperplasia (CAH) show the effect of large amounts of androgen
    - Girls with CAH, even with hormone therapy tend to prefer more masculine activities and may enlarge the clitoris to resemble a penis
    - CAH seems to affect the area of the brain involved in development of gender-role behavior

Evolving Gender Roles

- Family values and practices influence gender roles in children
- Historical influences and lifestyles of families may play a role
- Some gender roles do not seem as affected by these influences as others, possibly due to women giving birth and the necessity for caring and nurturing as part of the female gender role

Chapter Six
Off to School: Cognitive and Physical Development in Middle Childhood

6.1 Cognitive Development

Learning Objectives

- What are the distinguishing characteristics of thought during Piaget's concrete-operational and formal-operational stages?
- How do children use strategies and monitoring to improve learning and remembering?

More Sophisticated Thinking

- Piaget's Version
  - The Concrete-Operational Period
    - School-age children can perform mental operations – actions that can be performed on objects or ideas that have a consistent result
    - Thinking is bound to the concrete, here and now. Cannot deal effectively with abstract or hypothetical
- The Formal Operational Period
  - Around 11 years, children can reason abstractly
  - Adolescents may use deductive reasoning
  - Formal operations children understand that a hypothetical situation may not correspond to a real-world problem

Cognitive Development

- Comments on Piaget's View
  - Adolescents who are in the formal operational stage may not always reason at that level
  - Adolescents' thinking is often egocentric and irrational
  - Other theorists have pointed out that cognitive development continues after reaching the formal operational stage, contrary to Piaget's description

Information-Processing Strategies for Learning and Remembering

- Most human thinking takes place in working memory where only a small number of thoughts or ideas are stored for a short time
- Information may be transferred to long-term memory, which is permanent and unlimited in capacity

Memory Strategies

- 7- to 8-year-olds use rehearsal in which they repeatedly name the thing to be remembered
- As children mature, they develop strategies that are useful for specific situations such as organization and elaboration
- Even older children may sometime use an ineffective strategy in a situation

Metacognition

- Monitoring
  - Gradually, children learn about their own memory processes and begin to evaluate them
  - Elementary school-aged children can often identify information which they have not learned, but do not focus their attention on learning it
- Metamemory - a child's understanding of memory
- Metacognitive knowledge - awareness of one's own cognitive processes
- Cognitive self-regulation - selecting strategies and monitoring adequately

6.2 Aptitudes for School

Learning Objectives

- What is the nature of intelligence?
- Why were intelligence tests first developed? What are their features?
- How well do intelligence tests work?
- How do heredity and environment influence intelligence?
- How and why do test scores vary for different racial and ethnic groups?

Theories of Intelligence

- Psychometricians are specialists trained in psychological measurement in areas such as intelligence and personality
- Such professionals administer tests to large groups of people to look for common factors that may explain abilities
- Analysis has led to different conclusions about intelligence such as:
  - Spearman claimed intelligence is a general factor (g-factor) that affects all aspects of ability
  - Thurstone believed that intelligence was actually many (7) different and distinct abilities

The Hierarchical View of Intelligence

- Carroll postulated that intelligence may have different levels
- Factor g is the top category, with eight subcategories below

Gardner's Multiple Intelligences

- Based on Piaget and information-processing theories
- Recognizes 9 types of intelligences
- Emphasizes that development is not simultaneous in all areas
- Takes into consideration that the brain has different regions that have specific abilities

Chapter Six

Emotional Intelligence

- Daniel Goleman
  - The ability to use one's own and others' emotions effectively for solving problems
- Perceiving emotions accurately
- Regulating one's emotions

Sternberg's Theory of Successful Intelligence

- How do people achieve personal goals?
  - Analytic ability- One analyzes problems and comes up with solutions
  - Creative ability- Involves dealing adaptively with new situations and problems
  - Practical Ability- Understanding what will work

Binet & the Development of Intelligence Testing

- In 1904 the French government asked Alfred Binet and Theophile Simon to develop a method for identifying children who could not learn in traditional ways
- Binet & Simon developed a test to measure children's mental age, or the level at which they solved problems
- This first intelligence test was believed to distinguish between "bright" and "dull" children

The Stanford Binet

- Lewis Terman at Stanford University adapted Binet & Simon's test
- Terman created the intelligence quotient (IQ) which compared the mental age to the chronological age of children
  - IQ = MA/CA X 100

Intelligence Testing

- IQ tests no longer use the MA/CA comparison for computation of IQ
- Today, children's performance on tests are compared with data of other children their age
  - An IQ of 100 denotes average performance. Above 100 is above average. Below 100 indicates less than average performance

Contemporary IQ Tests

- The Stanford Binet V - The current (2003) version of Binet's test
- The Wechsler Intelligence Scale for Children- 4th Edition (WISC-IV)
- The Kaufman Assessment Battery for Children, 2nd Edition (K-ABC-II)

Chapter Six

Do Tests Work?

- Two Issues in Evaluating IQ Tests
  - Reliability - are the scores on IQ tests consistent?
- Studies show scores on modern tests are relatively stable when repeatedly administered
  - Validity - do IQ tests really measure intelligence?
- IQ tests are moderately good predictors of performance in school and work

Increasing Validity With Dynamic Testing

- IQ tests traditionally measure the current level of knowledge and certain skills
- Dynamic testing involves direct observation of a child learning new material
  - Based on Vygotsky's concept of the zone of proximal development and scaffolding
- Dynamic testing is new and still under evaluation

Hereditary & Environmental Factors

- IQ scores are affected by both heredity and environment
- Heredity influences both IQ scores and changes that occur during development
- Adopted children's IQs where more similar to biological parents than adoptive parents
- Environmental influence is seen in the fact that children's IQ scores have risen over the past century

The Impact of Interventions

- Studies show Head Start is effective in increasing test scores
- Studies of other intervention programs suggest that intervention works in increasing IQ scores and reading and math levels
- While intervention is expensive, the economic and social consequences of poverty and unemployment cannot be overlooked

The Impact of Ethnicity and Social Class

- Studies show differences in scores among ethnic groups
  - Asian Americans have highest scores, followed by European Americans, Hispanic Americans, and African Americans
- These differences are impacted by socioeconomic status. However, economic disadvantage does not fully explain the difference

A Role for Genetics?

- While differences in IQ scores are observed between ethnic groups, heredity does not adequately explain these differences
- Most researchers agree that environmental influences are major factors in these differences
- The content of tests may reflect the cultural bias of the test-makers. Culture-fair intelligence tests are constructed to include only items that are common to many cultures

- Test-Taking skills have an impact on test scores. Test-taking skills may be different due to experience with taking standardized tests, which can reflect cultural differences
- Scores on IQ tests are intended to predict performance in academic achievement. While they are successful to a certain degree, children with low scores can be successful in school

Stereotype Threat

- *Stereotypes* lead to beliefs that a group lacks ability or skill in a particular domain
- *Stereotype Threat* may affect performance when a member of this group attempts these tasks
- Members of the group may come to consider themselves less capable and performance diminishes

Interpreting Test Scores

- It is important to remember that all tests reflect adaptation to a particular cultural context
- Most intelligence tests predict success in a school environment
- The average difference in IQ scores between ethic groups is relatively small when considering the overall range of scores for the groups

6.3 Special Children, Special Needs

Learning Objectives

- What are the characteristics of gifted and creative children?
- What are the different forms of mental retardation?
- What is a learning disability?
- What are the distinguishing features of hyperactivity?

Gifted and Creative Children

- Traditionally, an IQ score of 130 or higher was considered gifted
  - Today, definitions of giftedness are also likely to include talents in art, music, writing, and dance
- Exceptional talent seems to partly stem from a love of the subject, receiving inspiring instruction from an early age, and parents who support and nurture a child's talent

Creativity

- Creativity is often linked to divergent thinking, or thinking in novel or unusual directions
- Intelligence is more often associated with convergent thinking in which a specific conclusion is drawn from information given

Children With Mental Retardation

- Mental retardation is defined as substantially below-average intelligence and adaptive behavior. IQ below 70 on standardized tests
- 25% of mental retardation results from some biological or physical problem and is called organic mental retardation
- Familial mental retardation includes the lower end of the normal range of intelligence

Types of Mental Retardation

- Four levels of mental retardation:
  - Mild
  - Moderate
  - Severe
  - Profound
- More extreme forms (severe & profound) are usually organic

Learning Disabilities

- A child with a learning disability must have:
  - Difficulty in one or more academic subject
- Normal intelligence
  - The disability is not caused by some other condition (e.g., poor instruction, sensory deficits)
- Roughly 5% of school-aged children have learning disabilities. Reading disability is the most common

Attention-Deficit Hyperactivity Disorder

- Characteristics include overactivity, inattention, and impulsivity
- 3-5% of school-age children are diagnosed with ADHD
  - Boys outnumber girls by 3:1
- No evidence ADHD that is caused by food allergies, sugar, or poor home life
- Strong hereditary and biological components

6.4 Academic Skills

Learning Objectives

- What are the components of skilled reading?
- As children develop, how does their writing improve?
- How do arithmetic skills change during the elementary-school years? How do U.S. students compare to students from other countries?
- What are the hallmarks of effective schools and effective teachers?

Chapter Six

Reading

- Components of reading include:
  - Word recognition - the process of identifying a unique pattern of letters
  - Comprehension - the process of extracting meaning from a sequence of words
- Foundations of reading skill:
  - Knowledge of letter names
  - Phonological awareness - knowing sounds by letter combinations
- Recognizing words
  - Reading requires the child to recognize the word or be able to sound out the word
  - Children also use context to recognize words
- Comprehension improves when children recognize a sequence of words as:
  - Working memory increases
  - General knowledge increases
  - Through experience, children learn reading strategies
  - Children learn to monitor their comprehension

Writing

- Writing ability increases as:
  - The child gains greater knowledge about topics
  - Children develop knowledge-telling strategies as well as better knowledge-transforming strategies
  - They gain a better command of spelling, punctuation, and handwriting
  - They learn better use of proofreading and revising their work

Math Skills

- By 6 years of age, children solve simple addition by counting, usually on their fingers
- By 1st grade, children add and subtract by counting mentally
- By age 8 or 9, children know addition tables and can add single digits by memory

Comparing U.S. Students with Students in Other Countries

- U.S. children do not perform in math as well as children from many other countries
- Children in Japan and Taiwan spend 50% more time in school than U.S. students
- U.S. students spend less time on homework
- American parents are more satisfied with their children's performance in school
- American parents believe ability is more the key to success
- Asian parents consider effort more imortant than native ability

Effective Schools, Effective Teachers

- U.S. schools are locally run. Great disparity exists between their success
- Research has identified characteristics of successful schools:
  - Staff and students understand excellence is the primary goal of the school
  - The school is safe and nurturing
  - Parents are involved
  - Progress of students, teachers, and programs is monitored

Teacher-Based Influences

- Students often associate teacher effectiveness with personality features such as caring and warmness
- Higher achievement is associated with:
  - Good classroom management
  - Taking responsibility for students' learning
  - Emphasizing mastery of topics
  - Active teaching
  - Attention to pacing
  - Valuing tutoring
  - Teaching students to monitor their own learning

6.5 Physical Development

Learning Objectives

- How much do school-age children grow?
- How do motor skills improve during the elementary school years?
- Are American children physically fit?
- What are the consequences of participating in sports?

Growth

- Boys and girls are about the same size for most of these years
- Girls are more likely to enter puberty toward the end of the elementary school years
- At ages 11-12, the average girl is about ½ inch taller than the average boy

Development of Motor Skills

- Children at 11 can throw a ball 3 times farther than at 3, and jump twice as far
- Fine motor skill improvement is obvious in handwriting

Gender differences in motor skills

- Fine motor skills such as handwriting tend to be better in girls
- Girls' flexibility and balance are better than boys
- Boys do better on strength tasks
- Girls may spend less time on sports and fitness-related activities
- Fitness activities provide practice for motor skills

Chapter Six

Participating in Sports

- Sports teach skills such as working as a part of a group
- Children in sports use new cognitive skills for playing strategies
- Adults sometimes overemphasize competition instead of skill development

American Youth Soccer Organization Code for Coaches

- Coach positively: Praise, don't criticize
- Be sure children have fun
- Have realistic expectations and demands
- Develop children's respect for opponents, coaches, referees, and the game
- Be a good role model for children

Chapter Seven
Expanding Social Horizons: Socioemotional Development in Middle Childhood

7.1 Family Relationships

Learning Objectives

- What is a systems approach to parenting?
- What are the primary dimensions of parenting? How do they affect children's development?
- What determines how siblings get along? How do first-born, later-born, and only children differ?
- How do divorce and remarriage affect children?
- What factors lead children to be maltreated?

The Family as a System

- Older views saw child development as primarily the result of parents' actions
- Current views of child rearing view the family as a system with parents and children affecting each other
- In addition, the family system is impacted by outside influences such as extended family, community, and even larger entities

Dimensions & Styles of Parenting

- Parenting can be viewed through the dimension of warmth and responsiveness
  - Children of warm parents feel secure, happy, and are more well-behaved
  - Children of hostile or uninvolved parents may be anxious and less controlled
- The dimension of control affects parenting effectiveness
  - Children of over-controlling parents may feel unable to develop standards of behavior on their own
- A balance of good control, communication, and warmth results in children with an understanding of what is expected and invites dialogue

Chapter Seven

Parenting Styles

- Authoritarian parenting combines high control with little warmth
  - Hard work, respect, and obedience are encouraged. There is little give-and-take and parents do not explain their decisions
- Authoritative parenting combines more control with warmth and responsiveness
  - They explain rules and encourage decision
- Indulgent-permissive parenting provides warmth with little control
  - Use little punishment and accept their children's behavior
- Indifferent-uninvolved parenting involves little warmth or control
  - Parents are not involved with their children except to provide for basic physical and emotional needs. They minimize their time with their children
- Styles of parenting have different effects on children's development
  - Authoritative parents' children tend to be more responsible, self-reliant, and friendly
  - Authoritarian parents' children have lower self-esteem and are less skilled socially
  - Children of indulgent-permissive parents are often impulsive and easily frustrated
  - Children of indifferent-uninvolved parents often have low self-esteem, and are aggressive, impulsive, and moody

Variations Associated with Culture and Socioeconomic Status

- European-American parents tend to value warmth and moderate control in order to encourage independence and self-reliance
- In Asian and Latin American countries, individualism is not as highly valued, and cooperation and collaboration are encouraged by more emotional restraint and control

Parental Behavior

- Parents who use direct instruction tell children what to do, and when and why
  - Most powerful when combined with modeling
- Learning by observation is effective, especially if paired with counterimitation, or learning what should not be done

Chapter Seven

Feedback

- The negative reinforcement trap occurs when a child cries, complains, or whines until the parent relents and provides what the child desires
- Punishment is most effective when it is
  - Immediate
  - Consistent
  - Informative (providing an explanation and a way to avoid it in the future)
  - Administered by a person with whom the child has a warm and affectionate relationship

Punishment

- Has side-effects and drawbacks, such as being only temporarily effective
- Children, upset by punishment, may not understand the purpose of the consequence
- Physical punishment may result in aggression as a means to resolve disputes with other children
- Time-out, a consequence of misbehavior in which the child sits alone in a boring location, is brief, effective, and informative

Influences of the Marital System

- Research demonstrates that chronic parental conflict is harmful to children
  - Jeopardizes children's feelings of a stable family
  - Affects the parent-child relationship
  - Parents in conflict may be too preoccupied for high quality parenting

Children's Contributions: Reciprocal Influence

- Children's characteristics affect how parents treat them
  - Age
  - Temperament and behavior

Siblings

- As families grow, sibling relationships become more complex
  - Toddlers talk more to mothers than to older siblings
  - By 4- years old, children talk more to older siblings than to mothers
  - One effect of a sibling's birth is that fathers interact more with older children
- The birth of another child is stressful and may result in withdrawal or regression (acting more immature)

Chapter Seven

Adopted Children

- 2-4% of U.S. children are adopted
- Adopted children are more likely to be prone to conduct disorders and adjustment problems in school
- These problems are more likely the older the child's age at the time of adoption, and is related to the quality of care before adoption
- Most adopted children do quite well

Impact of Birth Order

- First-Born Children
  - Parents are enthusiastic but inexperienced
  - Parents are demanding and have high expectations
  - Often have higher IQ scores, are more conforming, and are more likely to go to college
- Later-Born Children
  - Are less concerned about pleasing parents
  - Are more popular with peers and more innovative
- Only Children
  - Contrary to myth, are not more spoiled or egotistical
  - Succeed more often in school and have higher levels of IQ, leadership, autonomy, and maturity

Divorce and Remarriage

- In the 1990s, 50% of all U.S. children experienced their parents' divorce
- After divorce, children tend to live with mothers
- In research, mothers were less affectionate with children in the first months after divorce
- Parents were less able to control their children
- 2 years after divorce, mothers were more affectionate and better able to discipline
- 6 years after divorce, mothers and daughters were closer, with mothers and sons in conflict

What Aspects of Children's Lives are Affected by Divorce?

- Research shows that school achievement, conduct, adjustment, self-concept, and parent-child relations faired poorly compared to children of intact families
- Adolescents of divorced parents are more likely to become teen parents and to become divorced themselves
- There is a small, but significant increase in emotional problems of adult children of divorced parents

Chapter Seven

Impact of Divorce on Children

- Development may be affected by loss of a parent role model, economic hardship, and parental conflict
- Children are more affected during childhood and adolescence than preschool or college ages
- Children who are more emotional may be more negatively impacted by divorce
- Reward with warmth, support, communication. Parental cooperation and same-sex custody are positive in their impact

Blended Families

- More than 2/3 of divorced men and women remarry, resulting in blended families
- While school-age boys benefit from presence of a stepfather, girls do not adjust well to their mother's remarriage
- Research on children living with remarried father is sparse. Usually results in behavior problems, with children less likely to adjust well

Parent-Child Relationships Gone Awry: Child Maltreatment

- Physical Abuse - assault leading to physical injuries
- Sexual Abuse - fondling, intercourse, or other sexual behaviors
- Psychological Abuse - ridicule, rejection, or humiliation
- Neglect - inadequate food, clothing, or medical care

Who Are the Abusing Parents?

- Some countries' culture does not allow for physical punishment. Countries that have a culture that allows for spanking have higher rates of maltreatment
- The stress of poverty is correlated with abuse as is social isolation
- Infants, preschoolers, and frequently ill children are more often abused

Effects of Abuse on Children

- Abused children tend to have poor peer relationships
- Children of abuse do poorly in school
- Adults who were abused as children experience more depression and anxiety and are more likely to abuse their children

Preventing Abuse & Maltreatment

- Reducing physical punishment can help
- Maintaining social supports can give parents opportunities for venting and advise
- Counseling and parenting skills training can help

7.2 Peers

Learning Objectives

- What are the benefits of friendship?
- What are the important features of groups of children and adolescents? How do these groups influence individuals?
- Why are some children more popular than others? What are the causes and consequences of being rejected?
- Why are some children aggressive? Why are others frequent targets of aggression?

Friendships

- By 4-8 years, children single out specific peers as playmates
- At 8 or 9, children have their first intimate and reciprocal relationships
- Older children and adolescents emphasize loyalty in friendships
- By about 14, friendships consist of intimacy and support during stressful periods. Less dependence on family

Who Are Friends?

- Friends tend to be same-sexed, similar aged, and from the same race or ethnic group
- Friends tend to have similar interests, attitudes, and recreational pursuits
- Children with same-sexed and opposite-sexed friends tend to be more popular, well- adjusted, academically successful, and have higher self-esteem than those with same-sexed only friends

Quality and Consequences of Friendships

- Children with good friends tend to have higher self-esteem and are less likely to be lonely or depressed
- Friends, particularly girls, spend much of their time talking about each other's problems, which is known as co-rumination
- Children with good friends are more likely to engage in prosocial behavior
- Adults who had good friends as children experience greater feelings of self-worth

Groups

- Cliques tend to dress, talk, and act alike
- Members of cliques may become affiliated with others with similar values and attitudes called crowds
- Some crowds have more status than others and may impact self-esteem
- Parenting style and involvement may have impact on which crowd children affiliate with

Group Structure

- Often exhibit a dominance hierarchy with a leader and followers
- With boys, physical power is often the characteristic most often associated with leadership

- Among girls and older boys, individual traits that relate to the group's main interests determine leadership

Peer Pressure
- Irresistible pressure to conform to the group's norms
- Most junior-high and high-school students resist negative peer pressure
- Peer pressure is most effective when standards are not clear-cut. Subjective standards such as taste in music and clothing are examples. Also true for smoking, drinking, and drug usage

Popularity and Rejection
- Popular children are liked by classmates
- Rejected children are disliked by classmates
- Controversial children are both liked and disliked by classmates
- Average children are liked and disliked but without as much intensity
- Neglected children are ignored by classmates

Consequences of Rejection
- Rejected children are more likely to:
  - drop out of school
  - commit juvenile offenses
  - suffer from psychopathology

Causes and Consequences of Rejection
- Parental behavior can result in imitation of poor social skills and conflict
- Inconsistent punishment may result in aggressive and antisocial behavior

Aggressive Children and Their Victims
- When a child uses aggression to achieve an explicit goal, it is called instrumental aggression
- Aggression that is unprovoked and is used to intimidate or harass is called hostile aggression
- Children's tendency to behave aggressively is stable over time, especially if seen at a young age
- About 10% of elementary-school-age children and adolescents are chronic victims of aggression
- Children who are frequent victims are often lonely, anxious, depressed, and dislike school
- Victimized children may be aggressive themselves or tend to be withdrawn and submissive

7.3 Television: Boob Tube or Window on the World?
Learning Objectives
- What is the impact of watching television on children's attitudes and behavior?
- How does TV viewing influence children's cognitive development?
- How truthful are common criticisms of TV?

Influence on Attitudes &Social Behavior
- Research shows frequent viewing of TV violence increases aggressive behavior

- 8-year-olds that were exposed to large amounts of TV violence had more extensive criminal records as 30-year-olds. Similar results were found for violent video games

Stereotypes

- Some research suggests that exposure to TV may promote the acceptance of gender, race, and ethnic stereotypes by children
- Shows on TV do not accurately portray the demographic texture of society. Minorities and women may be under-represented and gender roles may be exaggerated
- Children who are heavy consumers of TV may accept these misrepresentations as reality

Consumer Behavior

- Preschool children may perceive commercials as a form of entertainment
- By 8 or 9, children begin to understand that commercials are meant to be persuasive and may not always be truthful
- Children are affected by advertising, and studies show that most ask parents to buy items seen on TV

Guides for Children and TV Viewing

- Parents should set absolute rules concerning amount of TV to be watched
- Children should not watch TV out of boredom
- Adults should watch TV with children and discuss programs
- Parents should model good TV viewing, avoiding shows that are inappropriate for young viewers

Prosocial Behavior

- Children are more likely to act prosocially after watching brief films in which peers acted prosocially
- Programs such as Mr. Rogers' Neighborhood were found to be effective in encouraging prosocial behavior, particularly in boys
- While these studies show that TV can promote prosocial behavior, children may not watch the appropriate shows, which are limited in number

Influences on Cognition

- Studies show that shows such as Sesame Street promote more proficiency at recognizing letters, numbers, counting, and vocabulary
- These studies confirm that TV can be a positive influence on these abilities if parents promote good viewing

Criticisms of TV

- Two major criticisms:
  - TV promotes short attention spans because of high-interest short segments
  - TV promotes passive, lazy thinkers who are less creative

- Findings:
  - No support for TV promoting short attention spans
  - Mixed findings on TV having negative impact on thinking and creativity

7.4 Understanding Others

Learning Objectives

- As children develop, how do their descriptions of others change?
- How does understanding of others' thinking change as children develop?
- When and why do children develop prejudice toward others?

Describing Others

- By 7-years-old, children describe others in concrete terms. By 10, they use more psychological traits. At 16-years, descriptions are integrated into a cohesive account
- Children's descriptions begin to help them to predict how others will behave

Understanding What Others Think

- Selman's Five Stages of Perspective Taking
  - Undifferentiated (3-6 years old)
  - Social-Informational (4-9 years old)
  - Self-Reflective (7-12 years old)
  - Third-Person (10-15 years old)
  - Societal (14 years to adult)

Research Findings on Selman's Theory

- Findings support prediction that children move through stages of development of perspective-taking
- Children at higher stages of cognitive development are at higher levels of perspective taking
- Children who are more advanced in perspective-taking are more well-liked by peers

Prejudice

- When children learn that they belong to a particular group, they learn prejudice
  - While prejudice decreases during elementary school, it increases again during adolescence
  - Children tend to view members of groups as more homogenous than they really are
  - Prejudice may be related to social status. The higher the status of the group, the more positive it is viewed
  - Prejudice may be reduced by discussions and role-play

Chapter Eight
Rites of Passage: Physical and Cognitive Development in Adolescence

8.1 Pubertal Changes

Learning Objectives

- What physical changes occur in adolescence that mark the transition to a mature young adult?
- What factors cause the physical changes associated with puberty?
- How do physical changes affect adolescents' psychological development?

Signs of Physical Maturation

- Puberty consists of two changes that mark the change from childhood to young adulthood
  - Dramatic increases in height, weight, and body fat distribution
  - Changes in the reproductive organs that mark sexual maturity, as well as secondary sexual characteristics such as body and facial hair, and the growth of breasts

Physical Growth

- During the adolescent growth spurt females gain as much as 20 pounds a year and boys 25 pounds
- Girls begin the growth spurt about 2 years before boys
- Girls start the growth spurt at about age 11 and reach mature stature at 15
- Boys begin at about 13 and reach mature stature at about 17

Brain Growth in Adolescence

- By the beginning of adolesence the brain is 95% of adult size and weight
- Myelination and synaptic pruning are nearly complete

Sexual Maturation

- Primary sex characteristics are the organs of reproduction
- Secondary sex characteristics denote physical signs of maturity that are not directly linked to reproduction. They include the breasts and the width of the pelvis in girls, and facial hair and broadening of shoulders in boys
- Menarche is the onset of menstruation in girls
  - First menstrual cycles are usually irregular and without ovulation
- Spermarche is the first spontaneous ejaculation of sperm-containing fluid
  - First ejaculations usually contain few sperm. Sufficient sperm to fertilize an egg may take months or years to develop

Chapter Eight

Mechanisms of Maturation

- The hypothalamus produces hormones to the pituitary gland, triggering growth hormones
- The pituitary stimulates other glands to produce estrogen in girls and testosterone in boys
- The timing of puberty is genetically regulated and is affected by health and nutrition
- Menarche occurs earlier in countries where nutrition and health care are better

Psychological Impact of Puberty

- Body Image
    - Teenagers are very attentive to physical changes, which take place very rapidly and are dramatic
    - Girls are more critical of their appearance and are likely to be dissatisfied. Boys are more likely to be pleased

Response to Menarche and Spermarche

- Girls tend to be moderately pleased by first menstruation but irritated by the messiness. Usually share the news with mothers and friends right away
- Boys' reactions are less well documented. They are usually more pleased if they know about it beforehand. They rarely tell parents and friends

Moodiness

- Increase in hormone levels are associated with greater irritability and impulsivity, but not moodiness
- Moodiness has been found to be more associated with activities. Recreational activities are more associated with good mood and adult-regulated activities with negative mood

Rate of Maturation

- Rate of maturation may have significant consequences for adolescents
- Early maturation usually benefits boys, but not girls
- Early maturing girls had more negative feelings about their physical development, while boys tend to have more positive feelings

8.2 Health

Learning Objectives

- What are the elements of a healthy diet for adolescents? Why do some adolescents suffer from eating disorders?
- Do adolescents get enough exercise? What are the pros and cons of participating in sports in high school?
- What are common obstacles to healthy growth in adolescence?

Chapter Eight

Nutrition

- Teenagers need high caloric intake because of high growth and metabolism rates
  - Girls need approximately 2200 calories per day
  - Boys need around 2700 calories daily
- Most U.S. teens consume sufficient calories but not in balanced, nutritional meals
- In the U.S. 1 of every 7 children is overweight

Obese Youths Can Lose Weight

- Successful programs focus on eating habits and sedentary behavior
- Success is rooted in monitoring their eating, exercise, and sedentary behavior. Short-term goals are set in each area
- Parents are trained to help set realistic goals and to use behavioral principles in meeting them

Anorexia & Bulimia

- Anorexia is a disorder marked by an irrational fear of being overweight
  - Have distorted body image
  - As many as 15% of adolescents with anorexia die
- Bulimia consists of binge eating and purging by vomiting or with laxatives
  - Bingeing may occur as many as 30 times per week
  - Adolescents with bulimia cannot stop eating

Physical Fitness

- Adolescents rarely get enough exercise
- Many adolescents engage in organized sports. Many more boys participate than girls
- Sports have been shown to enhance self-esteem and initiative, as well as help learn about cooperation and team-work
- A problem associated with sports is drugs used to enhance performance. Steroids are used to enhance muscle size, strength and recovery from injury. As many as 5-10% of boys use steroids

Threats to Adolescent Well-Being

- 1 of 1000 U.S. adolescents dies yearly. Most from auto accidents or firearms
- Accidental deaths often stem from decisions to engage in higher risk behaviors
- Adolescents and adults reason-out risk similarly. However, the weight given to specific risks may vary greatly
- Adolescents may give greater weight to the social consequences of choices

Chapter Eight

8.3 Information Processing During Adolescence

Learning Objectives

- How do working memory and processing speed change in adolescence?
- How do increases in content knowledge, strategies, and metacognitive skill influence adolescent cognition?
- What changes in problem-solving and reasoning take place in adolescence?
- How Does Information Processing Improve in Adolescence?
- For information-processing theorists, adolescence is not a separate stage
- Instead, it is seen as a rapidly changing transition from childhood cognition to young adulthood
- Changes do take place in certain areas of cognitive development

Working Memory & Processing Speed

- Speed of cognitive processing and memory capacity both achieve adult levels during adolescence
- Adolescents process information very efficiently

Content Knowledge

- During adolescence, children become as knowledgeable as adults in certain domains
- This enhances performance in some areas and assists them in understanding and learning new areas

Strategies and Metacognitive Skill

- Adolescents become more skilled at recognizing and developing strategies for specific tasks and for monitoring the strategy for their effectiveness
- They may develop master plans for studying in school

Limits on Information Processing

- While information processing ability increases during adolescence, this may not mean that they use these abilities effectively
- Choices may play a role in effective processing
- Less mature cognitive processing may be used because it is easier

8.4 Reasoning About Moral Issues

Learning Objectives

- How do adolescents reason about moral issues?
- Is moral reasoning similar in all cultures?
- How do concern for justice and caring for other people contribute to moral reasoning?
- What factors help promote more sophisticated reasoning about moral issues?

Chapter Eight

Kohlberg's Theory

- In response to a story of a moral dilemma, children pass through these stages:
  - Preconventional Level - moral reasoning is based on external forces
    - Obedience orientation is believing that authority figures know what is right and wrong
    - Instrumental orientation consists of looking out for their own needs
  - Conventional Level - look to society's norms for moral guidance
    - In the interpersonal norms stage, children are guided by the aim of winning the approval of others
    - In the social system morality stage, adolescents believe that social roles, expectations, and laws are for the good of all people
  - Postconventional Level - morals are based on a personal moral code
    - In the social contract stage, laws and expectations are good as long as they benefit all group members
    - At the universal ethical principles stage, people choose ethical principles such as justice, compassion, and equality

Support for Kohlberg's Theory

- Kohlberg wrote that people progress through the stages in only the order listed
- Longitudinal studies show that people do not skip stages and do not regress
- Research demonstrates links between levels of moral reasoning and moral action
  - Higher levels are associated with causes and following beliefs. Lower levels are associated with delinquency

Cultural Differences in Moral Reasoning

- Kohlberg's theory stresses higher level's emphasis on individual rights and justice, reflecting western Judeo-Christian values
- The principles reflected in other cultures may be different and affect resolutions of moral dilemmas
- Eastern cultures put caring for others and familial obligations above individual rights

Chapter Eight

Beyond Kohlberg's Theory: Carol Gilligan's Theory

- Gilligan argues that Kohlberg's emphasis on justice is more applicable to men than women, even in the western cultures
- The primary emphasis for women is caring. The highest principle is for the alleviation of social and global problems
  - Stage One - preoccupation with one's own needs
  - Stage Two - caring for others
  - Stage Three - emphasis of caring in all human relationships and denunciation of violence/exploitation

Promoting Moral Reasoning

- Children advance through contact with those at higher stages
- Kohlberg found that discussion of morality can help children see short-comings in moral reasoning

Chapter Nine
Moving into the Adult Social World: Socioemotional Development in Adolescence

9.1 Identity & Self-Esteem

Learning Objectives

- How do adolescents achieve an identity?
- What is an ethnic identity? What are the stages in acquiring an ethnic identity?
- How does self-esteem change in adolescence?

The Search for Identity

- Adolescents use hypothetical reasoning with other advanced cognitive skills to explore different roles and experiment with identity
- Much of the experimentation and thinking is related to careers
- Imagination and fantasy may be employed to consider the roles of talent, religion, morality, and economics in their identity
- Marcia's Four Different Identity Statuses
  - Diffusion - confusion and little progress
  - Foreclosure - status determined by adults, not by personal exploration
  - Moratorium - exploring alternatives but not yet found one that's satisfactory
  - Achievement - has deliberately chosen identity
- Adolescents are self-absorbed, which is referred to as adolescent egocentrism
- Imaginary audience - adolescents' feeling that they are watched constantly, like actors
- Adolescents feel that their experiences and feelings are unique and that no one has ever felt as they do. This is called the personal fable
- A common characteristic is the illusion of invulnerability - misfortune only happens to others

Ethnic Identity

- Developing a feeling of belonging, and learning the customs and culture of one's ethnic group
- Phases include:
  - Haven't examined their ethnic roots
  - Beginning to explore the personal impact of their ethnic heritage
  - Development of a distinct ethnic self-identity

Immigrant Adolescents

- Have a special challenge in carrying forward their cultural heritage while adjusting to an unfamiliar culture
- May have already established a strong identity associated with their country of origin
- Adolescents with strong ethnic identity have higher self-esteem and perform better in school

Identity and Ethnicity

- As each generation becomes more acculturated, identification with ethnic culture may lessen
- Adolescents from parents who come from mixed cultures, racial, or ethnic groups may have more challenges

Self-Esteem in Adolescence

- While self-esteem tends to be high in early elementary years, it may decline when children move to new schools and levels of education
- Self-esteem may not be consistent across academic, behavioral, and social domains. There may be differences between boys and girls as well

Influences on Adolescents' Self-Esteem

- Parental discipline plays a role. Parents who set rules but are willing to discuss rules promote high self-esteem
- School experiences affect self-esteem. Avoidance of discipline problems, working hard, and getting along with peers are factors correlated with higher self-esteem

The Myth of Storm and Stress

- Movies and books insinuate that adolescence is a time of storm and stress
- Research actually finds that most adolescents:
  - Admire and love their parents
  - Rely on parent's advice
  - Embrace many of their parents' values
  - Feel loved by their parents

9.2 Romantic Relationships and Sexuality

Learning Objectives

- Why do teenagers date?
- Why are some adolescents sexually active? Why do so few use contraceptives?
- What determines an adolescent's sexual orientation?
- What circumstances make date rape especially likely?

Romantic Relationships

- About 50% of 15-year-olds and 70% of 18-year-olds had romantic relationships in the past 1 ½ years
- Relationships may provide companionships, sexual exploration, or support
- Early dating with many partners is associated with problems in adolescence
- Early dating may be related to less satisfying romantic relationships in adulthood

Dating

- The first step toward romantic relationships consists of activities involving mixed groups of boys and girls
- Next, several pairs of boys and several girls go out together as a group
- Couples initially involve companionship and later trust and support
- Cultural factors affect dating patterns

Chapter Nine

Sexual Behavior

- Adolescents are less likely to engage in sex if they have close relationships with parents who discourage sex and monitor their activities
- Adolescents are more likely to have sex when their peers approve and they believe their friends are having sex
- Most adolescents have experienced sex by age 19, but with only one partner

Boys and Girls Have Different Attitudes

- Boys are more likely to describe their first partner as a casual date
- Girls report stronger feelings of love for first partners
- Boys have more positive feelings about their first experience
- Girls are more likely to experience feelings of guilt and fear

Sexually Transmitted Diseases

- Young adults account for 15% of all AIDS cases in the U.S.
- Most contracted the disease during adolescence
- Teenagers and young adults are more likely to engage in unprotected sex and to use intravenous drugs

Teenage Pregnancy and Contraception

- Roughly 1 in 11 U.S. teenaged girls become pregnant
- Several factors contribute to lack of use of contraceptives:
  - Ignorance - lack of information about conception
  - Illusion of invulnerability
  - Lack of motivation - becoming pregnant may seem attractive for some teens
  - Lack of access - Not knowing where or how to obtain contraceptives

Chapter Nine

Sexual Orientation

- About 15% of teens go through a period of emotional and sexual attraction to same-sex friends
- Around 5% of teens identify themselves as gay or lesbian
- False beliefs:
  - Sons become gay when raised by a domineering mother and a weak father
  - Girls become lesbians when their father is their primary role model
  - Children raised by gay or lesbian parents adopt their parents' orientation
  - Gay and lesbian adults were seduced by an older person of their sex
- Boys with older brothers are more often gay
  - Possible biochemical effect of producing male children
- Possible that hormones affect temperament, which may in turn affect behavior and feelings of being different
- In 1973 the official criteria manual for mental disorders dropped homosexuality as abnormal. This has reduced the stigma

Development of Same-Sex Attraction

- For males, attraction to other males may develop earlier
- For females attraction to other females more often occurs in late adolescence, middle, or old age
- Lesbians often first develop strong feelings for a specific woman and later, for other women

Sexual Coercion

- Several factors may be related to females being forced to have sex with someone they know, which is called date rape or acquaintance rape
  - Judgment or assertiveness impaired by alcohol
  - Provocative dress may send wrong signals
  - The fact that the couples have had sex before
- Factors related to boys committing acts of violence
  - Abused as children or witnessed domestic violence
  - Belief that violence is a normal part of romantic relationships

Guidelines for Communication Between Males and Females About Sex

- Know your sexual policies. When is sexual intimacy acceptable?
- Communicate these policies openly and clearly
- Avoid being alone with a person until you have discussed these policies
- Avoid use of alcohol and drugs when alone with someone with whom you don't want to be intimate
- Make your objections known. Talk first, but struggle and scream if necessary

Chapter Nine

9.3 The World of Work

Learning Objectives

- How do adolescents select an occupation?
- What is the impact of part-time employment on adolescents?

Career Development

- At about 13 or 14, a process called crystallization begins wherein adolescents consider their own talents and interests to start limiting their thinking about careers
- Around 18, adolescents begin learning more about certain lines of work and possibly begin training. This is called specification
- During implementation, adolescents enter the workforce and learn firsthand

Personality-Type Theory

- Holland proposed that people find work that fits their personality
- The Strong Interest Inventory (SII) obtains a person's scores on a number of characteristics and compares them with those of successful people in many occupations

Personality Types in Holland's Theory

- Realistic
- Investigative
- Social
- Conventional
- Enterprising
- Artistic

Part-Time Employment

- More than 15 hours of work weekly is associated with lower grades
- More than 15-20 hours a week are more likely to result in anxiety, depression, and lower self-esteem
- Part-time work does not usually teach the value of a dollar. Teens who work most often do not save, and spend most of their money on themselves for entertainment, snack food, and cosmetics
- When number of hours is kept lower, positive benefits are more likely to apply
- When jobs teach or take advantage of the child's skills, self-esteem may be enhanced
- When teens use their money for clothes, school expenses, and savings, parent-child relationships usually improve

9.4 The Dark Side

Learning Objectives

- Why do teenagers drink and use drugs?
- What leads some adolescents to become depressed? How can depression be treated?
- What are the causes of juvenile delinquency?

Chapter Nine

Drug Use

- Teenage Drinking
  - Why do adolescents drink?
- Experimentation, relaxation, escape
- Feelings of exhilaration
- Teenage Smoking
  - Teens usually begin between 6th and 7th grade
  - More likely to smoke if their parents smoke
  - More likely to smoke if their friends smoke

Depression

- Under 5% of early-to-mid adolescents are depressed. By late adolescence, 10% of boys and 25% of girls report being depressed
- Depressed adolescents prefer to be alone more than non-depressed adolescents
- Adolescents who feel that they are at the mercy of external events may experience learned helplessness, which is associated with depression
- Reduced levels of norepinephrine & serotonin may result in inability to experience pleasure

Treating Depression: Two Approaches

- Antidepressant drugs, such as the serotonin reuptake inhibitor Prozac, may help by treating the biological cause of depression
- Psychotherapy may be used to help learn social skills and to improve how they view their experiences

Preventing Teen Suicides

- While 10 in 100 adolescents report attempts at suicide, only 1 in 10,000 actually commit suicide
- More common in boys than girls
- More common among European American adolescents than African American. Native Americans have the highest rate of all ethnic groups
- Depression and/or drugs are often factors
- Common warning signs of suicide:
  - Threats of suicide
  - Preoccupation with death
  - Change in eating or sleeping habits
  - Loss of interest in activities that were once important
  - Marked changes in personality
  - Persistent feelings of gloom and helplessness
  - Giving away valued possessions

Delinquency

- Juvenile delinquency is illegal as well as destructive behavior toward themselves or others
- Status crimes are acts that are not crimes if exhibited by adults, such as truancy, sexual promiscuity, and running away from home
- Index crimes are illegal regardless of the age of the perpetrator

Chapter Nine

Causes of Delinquency

- Life-course persistent antisocial behavior emerges at an early age and continues throughout life
  - Often related to lower socioeconomic status, inadequate parental supervision, impulsivity, and a possible biological predisposition for aggressiveness in adolescents
- Adolescent-limited antisocial behavior is limited to minor criminal acts that are not consistently antisocial
  - May be more imitative and may attempt to achieve adult-like status

Treatment and Prevention

- Successful prevention programs usually include
  - Teaching effective self-control techniques
  - Teaching parents effective discipline and supervision skills
  - Developing better ways of resolving conflicts within families
  - School programs that encourage investment in school performance
  - Improvement of economic conditions in neighborhoods where delinquency is predominant

Chapter Ten
Becoming an Adult: Physical, Cognitive, and Personality Development

10.1 When Does Adulthood Begin?

Learning Objectives

- What role transitions mark entry into adulthood in Western societies? How do non-Western cultures mark the transition to adulthood?
- How does going to college fit in the transition to adulthood?
- What psychological criteria mark the transition to adulthood?
- What aspects of early young adulthood make it a separate developmental stage?

Role Transitions Marking Adulthood

- Role transitions in Western cultures
  - Role transitions are when individuals assume new responsibilities and duties, such as completing an education, marriage, and becoming a parent.
  - These transitions vary as to the age at which they occur. Historical variations are common

Cross-Cultural Evidence of Role Transitions

- Marriage is the most common non-Western transition that marks adulthood
- Non-Western cultures often have specific criteria for boys' transition to adulthood. These usually include aspects of being able to provide, protect, and impregnate
- Menarche is the most common marker for adulthood in girls

Role Transitions Marking Adulthood (Cont)

- Rites of passage are rituals that mark initiation into adulthood
- Rites may last minutes, hours, or days
- Tribal rituals may include pain or mutilation
- Certain ethnic groups rely on formal rites such as bar mitzvahs

Going to College

- Traditionally, people think of the ages of 18 through 25 as the college years
- The actual average age of college students in the U.S. is 29
- Students over the age of 25 are called returning adult students
- Returning students are often more highly motivated and study more than traditional students

Psychological Views

- Adulthood usually brings more self-control and a drop in reckless behavior
- Erikson's theory points out the importance of developing independence and the capacity for intimacy

Establishing Intimacy

- Erikson's stage of intimacy vs. isolation is the psychosocial challenge of young adulthood
- Identity development is critical for being able to achieve intimacy
- Research shows that some women resolve intimacy issues after their children have grown and moved away

So When Do People Become Adults?

- The ages between 18 and 25 are often considered a distinct life stage, sometimes called thresholders
- Individuals of this age group are often not adults in every sense, but are no longer adolescents
- 50% of college students expect to live with their parents again

10.2 Physical Development & Health

Learning Objectives

- In what respects are young adults at their physical peak?
- How healthy are young adults in general?
- How do smoking, drinking alcohol, and nutrition affect young adults' health?
- How does young adults' health differ as a function of socioeconomic status, gender, and ethnicity?

Growth, Strength, and Physical Functioning

- Height reaches its greatest during young adulthood and is stable until old age
- Physical strength in both sexes peaks in the late 20s and early 30s
- While visual acuity remains stable through middle age, hearing begins to decline in the late 20s

Health Status

- 90% of young adults say their health is good or better
- Death in the early 20s is relatively rare
- Accidents, followed by cancer, cardiovascular disease, suicide, and AIDS are the leading causes of death in the U.S. between the ages of 24 and 44

Lifestyle Factors

- Smoking
  - Smoking is the leading contributor to health problems
  - Nicotine is a known potent teratogen
  - Quitting smoking is usually beneficial, regardless of how or when it happens

Drinking Alcohol

- Occasional drinking has not been shown to be a serious contributor to health problems
- Binge drinking is consuming 5 or more drinks in a row for men and 4 or more for women, within a 2 week period
- Binge drinking has been shown to be a major health concern, especially among college students

Chapter Ten

Nutrition

- Experts agree that nutrition affects mental, emotional, and physical functioning
- Metabolism, or how much energy the body needs, affects all areas
- Obesity is a factor in health problems
- Body mass index (BMI) is a ratio of body weight and height, and is recommended to be less than 25

Social, Gender, and Ethnic Issues in Health

- Social Factors
  - People in poverty are less likely to obtain adequate health care and are more often in poor health
  - People with better income as a result of education are less likely to be ill and less likely to die from chronic illness
- Gender
  - Women live longer than men and use health services more often

Ethnic Group Differences

- In the U.S. the residents of inner-city neighborhoods have the poorest health conditions
- African American men in large urban areas have lower life expectancy
  - Poverty plays a major role
  - Racism may play a role

10.3 Cognitive Development

Learning Objectives

- What is intelligence in adulthood?
- What types of abilities have been identified? How do they change?
- What is postformal thought? How does it differ from formal operations?
- How do stereotypes influence thinking?

How Should We View Intelligence in Adults?

- Most theories are multidimensional, though there is little agreement as to what the dimensions are
- Adults' intelligence is multidirectional in that some aspects improve while others decline during adulthood
- Interindividual variability shows that patterns of change vary between people
- Abilities show plasticity in that they may be modified during any point in adulthood, under the right conditions

What Happens to Intelligence in Adulthood?

- Primary mental abilities include:
  - Number
  - Word fluency
  - Verbal meaning
  - Inductive reasoning
  - Spatial orientation

Chapter Ten

Secondary Mental Abilities

- Fluid intelligence is the ability to be a flexible thinker
  - Used in puzzles, mazes, and relations among shapes. Declines throughout adulthood
- Crystallized intelligence is knowledge acquired by life experience
  - The ability to remember historical facts, definitions, and sports trivia. This improves throughout adulthood

Going Beyond Formal Operations

- Thinking in Adulthood
  - Piaget's theory placed adolescents and adults in the formal operations stage
  - Other researchers have found differences in how adolescents and adults process information

Thinking in Adulthood

- Postformal thought consists of thinking that solutions must be realistic and that things are often not clear-cut
- Kitchener & King have described the stages of development of reflective judgment including phases of:
  - Optimal level of development which is the highest level of thinking of which a person is capable
  - Skill acquisition is the gradual, haphazard process of learning new abilities

Integrating Emotion and Logic in Life Problems

- Part of postformal thinking is the recognition that individuals' experiences differ and will therefore result in different ways of thinking about things
- In postformal thinking there is a recognition of the importance of emotion integrated with logic in decision-making
- This results in an appreciation for the need for compromise and tolerance

The Role of Stereotypes in Thinking

- Stereotypes are examples of how social knowledge structures and social beliefs can shape our thinking and perceptions
- Stereotypes affect how we interpret new information
- Implicit stereotypes are beliefs that we may not be aware of, but may affect our behavior
- Stereotype threat is the fear of being judged by a negative stereotype about a group to which one belongs

Implicit Social Beliefs

- We may be able to determine the importance of age-related social belief if we examine:
- The content of the beliefs
- The strength of these beliefs
- The likelihood that these beliefs will be activated automatically when they are questioned or violated

Chapter Ten

10.4 Who Do You Want to Be? Personality in Young Adulthood

Learning Objectives

- What is the life-span construct? How do adults create scenarios and life stories?
- What are possible selves? Do they show differences during adulthood?
- What are personal control beliefs?

Creating Scenarios and Life Stories

- Young adults create a life-span construct, or view of the past, present, and future
- The construct is manifested in a scenario, or expectations about the future
- The social clock is the expectation that future events will correspond to a certain age or date
- We construct a life story as we begin to achieve some of the goals of our scenario. The story ties events together in a coherent sequence

Possible Selves

- Young adults tend to think of possible selves, or what we could become, would like to become, and are afraid of becoming
- In later life the possible selves are projected into fewer domains
- Health takes on more importance as a feared self as adults age

Self-Concept

- Self-concept is a result of integrating the scenario or life story into a sense of self
- In longitudinal studies, this self-concept did not appear to be modified by age beyond young adulthood
- Self-concept influences how people interpret experiences which, in turn, further shapes and defines their sense of identity

Personal Control Beliefs

- Personal control beliefs reflect the degree to which one believes that their performance depends on something they do
- These beliefs seem to have a great influence on our behavior
- Researchers have proposed four types of control:
  - Control from within oneself
  - Control over oneself
  - Control over the environment
  - Control from the environment
- How control beliefs are changed over the course of development is not clear
- Developmental changes vary over different domains (e.g., health, intelligence, etc.)
- Primary control is behavior aimed at affecting the external world
- Secondary control is behavior or thinking that is intended to affect the internal world

Chapter Eleven
Being with Others: Forming Relationships in Young and Middle Adulthood

11.1 Relationships

Learning Objectives

- What type of friendships do adults have? How do adult friendships develop?
- What is love? How does it begin? How does it develop through adulthood?
- What is the nature of violence in some relationships?

Friendships

- Adult friendships develop over several stages
  - Acquaintanceship
  - Buildup
  - Continuation
  - Deterioration
  - Ending
- Young adults tend to have more friends than during any other stage of adulthood
- Research suggests that satisfaction with life is partly dependant upon the quantity and quality of contact with friends
- Friendships usually encompass three themes:
  - Affective or emotional: Self-disclosure and trust
  - Shared or communal nature: Mutual interests
  - Sociability and compatibility: Source of fun and entertainment
- Sibling friendships are important as well. More for women than for men

Men's, Women's and Cross-Sex Friendships

- Women tend to base friendships on more intimate sharing and confiding in others
- Men's friendships tend to be based on shared interests or activities
- Men's friendships tend to involve less sharing and more competition
- Women tend to have more close friends
- Cross-sex relationships may help men with their capacity for intimacy

Love Relationships

- Sternberg's three basic components of love:
  - Passion - physical desire
  - Intimacy - need to share thoughts and actions
  - Commitment - willingness to stay with someone during good and bad times

Chapter Eleven

Love Through Adulthood

- Early in relationships, passion tends to be high and intimacy and commitment lower. This is called infatuation
- Falling in Love
  - The theory of assortative mating suggests that people find partners based on similarity
  - Homogamy is the degree to which people are similar. Research found that greater homogamy was present between partners that met in school or some religious setting

Meeting and Falling In Love

- Meeting at school is likely to result in the highest level of homogamy
- Online dating has resulted in many couples meeting and forming committed relationships
- Research shows three factors that are important when people meet someone
  - Stimulus
  - Values
  - Role

Selection and Dating

- Studies find differences between women's preferences in the looks of the men they meet
  - More masculine for shorter term relationship
  - More feminine for husbands or someone their parents would want them to date

Couples and Culture: Mate Preferences

- There is great diversity in preferences across cultures
- Two main dimensions emerge:
  - Cultural values
  - The importance of education, intelligence, and social refinement
- Chastity was a highly variable characteristic
- World-wide, men preferred attractiveness and women valued the ability to be a good provider

Developmental Forces and Relationships

- Choices are influence by biopsychosocial factors
- Research shows the importance of the dopamine system in love
- Erikson describes the importance of the development of the capacity for intimacy for mature relationships

Chapter Eleven

The Dark Side of Relationships: Violence

- Abusive relationships may result in battered woman syndrome where a woman believes that she cannot leave an abusive situation. She may go as far at to kill her abuser
- Studies have found a continuum of aggressive behaviors toward a spouse
- Some violence, such as pushing or slapping, occurs in 25-40% of committed relationships
- Studies show that the complexity of the causes of abusive behavior increases as the severity increases
- Violence may start as common violence, or physical aggressiveness between the couple
- There may be patriarchal terrorism in which men systematically abuse women

11.2 Lifestyles

Learning Objectives

- Why do some people decide not to marry, and what are these people like?
- What are the characteristics of cohabiting people?
- What are gay and lesbian relationships like?
- What is marriage like through the course of adulthood?

Singlehood

- 70% of women and 80% of men are single between the ages of 20 and 24
- Men tend to remain single longer than women
- Twice as many African Americans as European Americans are single throughout adulthood
- Young adults may perceive married people as caring, kind, and giving

Being Single

- Single people receive less compensation at work
- Rental agents preferred married couples 60% of the time in a recent study

Cohabitation

- Three reasons for decision to cohabit
  - Part-time or limited cohabitation is usually for convenience and accessibility. No long term commitment, marriage is not a goal
  - Premarital cohabitation is usually a trial marriage and if it doesn't end in marriage, the couple splits-up
  - Substitute marriage is a long-term commitment without legal marriage and is more common with older couples who may lose financial benefits if they marry
- Research on cohabitation suggests that it does not increase the chances of a successful marriage, though more recent research shows lessening of the negative effect

Gay and Lesbian Couples

- Most research shows similar issues for marriages between homosexual and heterosexual couples
- Heterosexual couples argue more about financial, political, and social value issues
- Homosexual couples are more likely to argue about trust issues
- Gay and lesbian couples report less support from family than do married or cohabiting couples

Marriage

- Studies show the median age at which couples marry has been rising for the past several decades
- Women under the age of 20 at the time of their first marriage are 3 times more likely to divorce than women who marry in their 20s, and 6 times more likely than those in their 30s

What Factors Help Marriage Succeed?

- Teen marriages are more likely to end in divorce partly due to the need for the development of a strong sense of identity before intimacy
- Homogamy, or similarity of interests and values, increases the chance of successful marriage
- Exchange theory suggests that marriages are more likely to succeed if each partner provides something to the relationship that another would not be able to provide

Do Married Couples Stay Happy?

- Studies show that satisfaction with marriage is highest in the beginning, falls until children begin leaving home, and rises again in later life
- When dependence is more equal, marriage tends to stay strong and close
- When dependence is less equal, more conflict and difficulty is experienced

The Early Years

- Less educated couples experience greater dissatisfaction with their marriage
- Couples who do not pool their financial resources experience less satisfaction
- With the birth of children, marriages become more routine and static, resulting in less satisfaction. However, childless couples' satisfaction declines as well

Marriage at Midlife

- Couples who have grown apart but remain married are called married singles
- Physical appearance is an important factor in marital satisfaction. Declines in physical condition due to aging may cause changes in level of satisfaction with marriage

Chapter Eleven

Older Couples

- Satisfaction with marriage tends to be higher in older ages
- Relationships improve further shortly after retirement
- Declines in health and advancing age often leads to a decrease in marital satisfaction
- While the amount of past or present sexual activity or interest does not seem to be related to marital satisfaction, interaction with friends is

Keeping Marriages Happy

- Couples who have enjoyed happy marriages over the years are better able to deal with changes and challenges
- Problems an individual experiences may actually bring couples closer, except for physical illness which has a tendency to negatively affect marital quality
- The most important factors in good marriages are good communication about thoughts, feeling, and actions

Seven Keys to Staying Married

- Make time for your relationship
- Express your love to your spouse
- Be there in times of need
- Communicate about problems in the relationship
- Be interested in your spouse's life
- Confide in your spouse
- Forgive minor offenses, try to understand major ones

11.3 The Family Life Cycle

Learning Objectives

- Why do people have children?
- What is it like to be a parent? What differences are there in different types of parenting?

Deciding Whether to Have Children

- More than 50% of all pregnancies in the U.S. are unplanned
- Finances are always a big consideration
  - An average family having a child in 2000 will spend $241,770 over 17 years for food shelter and other necessities to raise a child
- Childless couples have higher standard of living and greater marital satisfaction, but may be viewed negatively by society

The Parental Role

- Couples are having fewer children and waiting longer
  - Older parents are more at ease, spend more time with their babies, are more affectionate
  - Men who become fathers in their 30s spend up to 3 times as much time caring for their preschool children
  - More than 70% of women with children under 18 are employed outside the home and still perform most of the child-rearing tasks

Ethnic Diversity and Parenting

- African American husbands are more likely to help with household chores and child care than European American husbands
- Native American families assign important roles to children, and tribal members spend large amounts of time passing cultural values on to them
- Latino families are less likely than European or Asian American families to be two-parent families
- Latino families value familism (placing the well-being of the family over individual concerns)

Single Parents

- Roughly 70% of African American births, 40% of Latino births, and 20% of European American births are out-of-wedlock
- Causes include high divorce rates, the decision to keep out-of-wedlock children, and fertility rates
- Divorced single parents report feelings of frustration, guilt, and a tendency to be overindulgent
- Single parents often face financial strains. Single mothers are often affected the most

Alternate Forms of Parenting

- One-third of North American couples become step, foster, or adoptive parents
- Many children remain very close to non-custodial parents
- Children of blended families have more mental health difficulties than non-divorced children
- Adopted children may wish to have contact with birth parents, which may be viewed as rejection by adoptive parents
- Foster parents have most difficulty developing and maintaining bonds with their foster children
  - Foster children vary in age at the time they were taken from biological parents
  - Foster children may be re-united with their parents, or adopted by another couple
- Research shows that children raised by gay and lesbian parents do not experience any more problems than those raised by heterosexual couples, there may be resistance to their having children
- 90% of sons of gay fathers are heterosexual
- Though controversy continues, studies show that lesbian couples show more awareness of parenting skills than heterosexual couples

11.4 Divorce and Remarriage

Learning Objectives

- Who gets divorced? How does divorce affect parental relationships with children?
- What are remarriages like? How are they similar to and different from first marriages?

Chapter Eleven

Divorce

- Who gets divorced and why?
  - Ethnicity is a big factor
    - African American, Puerto Ricans, and ethnically mixed marriages are most likely to end in divorce
    - European Americans, Mexican Americans, and Cuban Americans are similar in divorce rates

Divorce and Remarriage

- Reasons men give for divorce:
  - Communication problems
  - Unhappiness
  - Incompatibility
  - Sexual problems
  - Financial problems
  - Emotional abuse
  - Women's liberation
  - In-laws
  - Infidelity by spouse
  - Alcohol abuse by self
- Reasons women give for divorce:
  - Communication problems
  - Unhappiness
  - Incompatibility
  - Emotional abuse
  - Financial problems
  - Sexual problems
  - Alcohol abuse by spouse
  - Infidelity by spouse
  - Physical abuse
  - In-laws

Effects of Divorce on the Couple

- Typically divorced individuals feel disappointed, misunderstood, and rejected
- Divorced people often find it difficult to let go or to find new friendships
- People with less preoccupation with the divorced spouse adjust better to single life
- Men are more likely to feel shocked, be blamed for the break-up, accept the blame, move out, and therefore have their social life disrupted
- Women are usually at an economic disadvantage, have a more difficult time with prospects for remarriage, and are likely to have inadequate child support
- Middle-aged individuals may have the most difficult time after divorce because of friends taking sides and are less likely to remarry

Relationships with Young Children

- 90% of divorces are not contested and 70% of the time the mother is awarded custody
- Custody issues are among the most difficult on parents and children
  - 70% of the cases in which a father sues for custody are successful in attaining custody or partial custody
  - For financial reasons, fathers may be encouraged to sue for custody whether they actually want to have it or not

Relationships with Adult Children

- Even many years after the divorce, men are less likely than women to have positive relationships with their adult children
- Adult daughters' relationship with their mothers are more likely to be positive, or intensify, after the divorce

Remarriage

- On average, men and women wait about 4 years before remarrying
  - African Americans wait longer than European Americans or Hispanics
  - Remarriages have 25% higher rate of divorce than original marriages
  - Remarriages involving stepchildren are 3 times more likely to end in divorce
  - Women are more likely to initiate a divorce, but are less likely to remarry

Chapter Twelve
Work and Leisure: Occupational and Lifestyle Issues in and Middle Adulthood

12.1 Occupational Selection & Development

Learning Objectives

- How do people view work? How do occupational priorities vary with age?
- How do people choose their occupations?
- What factors influence occupational development?
- What is the relation between job satisfaction and age?

The Meaning of Work

- Most people work to make a living but also find meaning in their work
- Research has found that people have four common ways in which personal fulfillment is derived from work
  - Developing and becoming self
  - Union with others
  - Expressing self
  - Serving others

Holland's Theory of Occupational Choice Revisited

- People pursue careers that are a good fit between their abilities and interests
- Six personality types that combine these factors: investigative, social, realistic, artistic, conventional, and enterprising
- Holland's theory does not tell us much about the differences among ethnic groups or the match with personality type and occupational choices in adulthood

Occupational Development

- How we advance within chosen occupations depends on many factors including
  - Expectations
  - Support from coworkers
  - Priorities
  - Job satisfaction

Super's Theory

- People progress along a continuum of vocational maturity through five stages
  - Implementation stage
  - Establishment stage
  - Maintenance stage
  - Deceleration stage
  - Retirement stage
- Occupational aspirations at age 16 in the U.K. predicted occupational attainments at 33
- In the U.S., people change occupations several times during adulthood

Chapter Twelve

Occupational Expectations

- Research by Levinson has shown that there are several major life tasks for adults
  - Developing a dream is one of these tasks
- Changing interests and failure can be cause for changing the dream
- Leaving school and learning about the real world is often a time of reality shock for young adults

The Role of Mentors and Coaches

- More experienced workers often communicate the most critical kinds of information rather than formal training
- Mentors help young workers avoid trouble and explain the unwritten rules of the job
- Mentors often guide young workers and help to ensure that they are noticed and get credit from supervisors
- Kram described four phases of the mentoring relationship:
  - Initiation
  - Cultivation
  - Separation
  - redefinition

Job Satisfaction

- Job satisfaction tends to increase with age
  - Probably because with advancing age, workers tend to select and stay with jobs that satisfy them and move on from work that is less satisfying
- Middle-aged workers tend to be more satisfied with the intrinsic rewards of work than they are with extrinsic rewards such as pay
- As workers get older, work may not be as much of a focus of their lives
- People change how they go about their work and jobs, resulting in a cyclical pattern to job satisfaction

Alienation and Burnout

- Alienation - the feeling that what a worker is doing is meaningless, no relationship between what they do and the end product
- The personality trait of cynicism is the factor most related to alienation
- To reduce alienation, stay involved in the decision-making, develop flexible work schedules, and provide employee development
- Burnout – a depletion of a person's energy and motivation
  - Results from stress, emotional exhaustion, and diminished personal accomplishment
  - Can be avoided by stress-reduction techniques, lowering people's expectations of themselves, and enhancing communication with the organization

Chapter Twelve

12.2 Gender, Ethnicity, and Discrimination Issues

Learning Objectives

- How do women's and men's occupational expectations differ? How are people viewed when they enter occupations that are not traditional for their gender?
- What factors are related to women's occupational development?
- What factors affect ethnic minority workers' occupational experiences and occupational development?
- What types of bias and discrimination hinder the occupational development of women and ethnic minority workers?

Gender Differences in Occupational Selection

- Traditionally, boys have been trained to think about what work they will do and taught that men are known by the work that they do
- Boys are taught that a part of masculinity is occupational achievement, and through games, that it is important to be a good follower and team player
- Traditionally, girls have not been taught to value these factors as much as those of being supportive, quiet, and accommodating
- The increase in the participation of women's athletic programs has been helpful in changing this difference

Traditional & Nontraditional Occupations

- Women tend to select nontraditional occupations because of personal feelings, experiences, and expectations about the occupation
- Women who have both brothers and sisters and attended single-sex high schools are most likely to choose nontraditional occupations
- Women who rate high on tests of traditional measures of femininity choose more traditional occupations but may feel unchallenged
- Women in nontraditional occupations are still often viewed negatively by peers of either sex
- People often make assumptions about working conditions based on their perception of an occupation as traditionally masculine or feminine
- People are less likely to recognize sexual harassment of a female when she works in a nontraditional occupation

Women & Occupational Development

- Most important issues for women tend to be whether the work environment is supportive, lack of development opportunities, and organizational politics
- Women tend to leave their jobs for two reasons
  - Women may prefer to work interdependently with peers. Corporations that do not value this are negatively viewed
  - Women may feel disconnected from colleagues, clients, and coworkers, leaving them feeling alienated

Ethnicity and Occupational Development

- While African American and European American women do not differ in their plans to enter nontraditional occupations, African American women seek more formal training, becoming overqualified
- African American and European American men have higher vocational identity when they graduate from college versus European American women and Hispanic American men

Bias and Discrimination

- Gender Bias and the Glass Ceiling
  - Only 5% of senior managers in the Fortune 500 are women
  - The glass ceiling is a term referring to the promotional level above which women may not go
  - Women are paid, on average, ¾ of what men are paid in the same positions. Larger gaps are observed for Hispanic and African American women

Sexual Harassment

- Reports suggest that as few as 5% of victims of sexual harassment report it
- Studies have shown that as many as 40% of women have experience sexual harassment in the workplace
- Research shows that harassment results in negative emotional, mental health, and job-related outcomes

Age Discrimination

- Denying a job or promotion to an individual solely based on age is age discrimination
- Federal law prohibits this practice for workers over the age of 40
- Age discrimination is when a part of the job requirement is a type of performance that older workers are less likely to be rated high on
- Retirement incentives and stereotyped beliefs affecting job performance ratings are also common

12.3 Occupational Transitions

Learning Objectives

- Why do people change occupations?
- Is worrying about potential job loss a major source of stress?
- How does job loss affect the amount of stress experienced?

Chapter Twelve

Occupational Transitions

- The reasons people leave their jobs are varied
  - Unhappy with the work
  - Obsolete skills
  - Economic trends
  - Pursuing additional training or education
- Retraining Workers
  - Career plateauing occurs when there is a lack of opportunity or when a person decides not to seek advancement
  - The retraining of mid-career and older workers emphasizes the need for life-long learning

Occupational Insecurity

- Economic conditions in the U.S. have resulted in many people losing jobs
  - Many people experience feelings of insecurity
  - People who worry about their jobs tend to have poorer mental health and negative attitudes about their employer
  - Negative attitudes may result even if the anxiety over the job is not based on fact

Coping With Unemployment

- Unemployment often results in declines in physical health and self-esteem
- Middle-aged men are more susceptible to the negative effects of unemployment
- Unemployment rates are higher for ethnic minority groups than for European Americans. The stress involved affects all groups similarly
- Recommendations
  - Approach job loss with a healthy sense of urgency
  - Consider next career move and what must be done to achieve it, even if there are no prospects for it at the present
  - Admit and react to change as soon as you realize it is there
  - Be cautious of stop-gap employment
  - Identify a realistic goal and list the steps needed to achieve it

12.4 Work and Family

Learning Objectives

- What are the issues faced by people who care for dependents?
- How do partners view the division of household chores? What is work-family conflict? How does it affect couples' lives?

Chapter Twelve

The Dependent Care Dilemma

- Employed Caregivers Revisited
  - Many mothers have to return to work after the birth of a baby
  - Some women struggle with the issue of returning to work, weighing financial need and the need to care for their children
  - Some women feel the need to return to work as a result of attachment to their work

Employed Caregivers

- Giving up work means a redefinition of one's identity
- 65% of women caring for a parent or partner work at least 35 hours
- The need to care for a parent or partner along with the lack of availability of affordable help forces many out of the workforce

Dependent Care and Effects of Workers

- Women experience significant negative effects of being responsible for dependent care
- When responsible for the care of a parent, women report more missed meetings and more absences from work. Higher levels of stress results
- Stress is decreased by having partners who provide support and having a job that allows for control over one's work schedule

Dependent Care and Employer Responses

- Many governments provide government-supported child-care centers for employees
- Providing child-care support is important, but positive impact is more often seen when supervisors are supportive and benefits that employees consider important are provided
- Better job security, autonomy, lower productivity demands, supervisor support, and flexible schedules are helpful

Juggling Multiple Roles

- Dividing Household Chores
  - Women still spend up to 50% more hours per week than men in family work
  - Unequal division of labor is the greatest source of arguments and unhappiness in two-earner households
  - While men have increased the amount of time spent on household chores, the greatest amount of the increase is on the weekends

Dividing Household Chores

- Men are more satisfied with the division of household labor
- Women are more satisfied when men take on tasks that are traditionally women's chores
- African American and Hispanic men spend more time on household chores than European American men
- Across cultures studied, gender inequality was greatest for women employed full-time

Chapter Twelve

Work-Family Conflict

- Work and family roles do not necessarily affect each other all of the time
- Women are not as concerned about the amount of time men spend on household chores as when there are certain "women's chores" that men will not perform
- The division of household labor is often the result of people's experience with their parents' assignment of chores
- Studies suggest that women often cope successfully with careers and family and the stress involved
- The number of children, not the ages of the children, was found to be a significant factor in their success
- Highest level of stress was during the peak parenting years when there were often at least two preschool children in the home
- Dual-earner couples have difficulty finding time for each other
- The amount of time is not necessarily the most important issue as long as they enjoy the time together and it is spent in shared activities
- Cross-cultural data suggests that work and parenting-related burnout is more likely to affect women

12.5 Time to Relax: Leisure Activities

Learning Objectives

- What activities are leisure activities? How do people choose among them?
- What changes in leisure activities occur with age?
- What do people derive from leisure activities?

Types of Leisure Activities

- Leisure activities can be classified as
  - Cultural
  - Physical
  - Social
  - Solitary
- Other ways to distinguish between leisure activities
  - The degree of cognitive, emotional, or physical involvement
  - Preoccupation versus interests

Developmental Changes in Leisure

- Young adults participate in a greater range of activities
- Middle-aged adults are more concerned with home- and family-oriented, less physically strenuous activities
- There is a great deal of stability over developmental ages in leisure activities preferred

Chapter Twelve

Consequences of Leisure Activities

- Research shows that
  - Participation is related to well-being
  - Leisure activities promote mental health
  - Leisure activities lessen the effects of stress and negative life events
  - They strengthen feelings of attachment to one's partner, family, and friends
  - They may be used to explore interpersonal relationships
  - Leisure results in more marital satisfaction if spent with others rather than only as a couple

Chapter Thirteen
Making It in Midlife: The Unique Challenges of Middle Adulthood

13.1 Physical Changes and Health

Learning Objectives

- How does appearance change in middle age?
- What changes occur in bones and joints?
- What reproductive changes occur in men and women in middle age?
- What is stress? How does it affect physical and psychological health?
- What benefits are there to exercise?

Changes in Appearance

- In middle age, people begin to notice significant amounts of wrinkles, gray hair, and possibly baldness
- Most people gain weight between their 30s and middle 50s
- People have varying psychological reactions to signs of aging

Changes in Bones and Joints

- Loss of bone mass is a potentially serious problem in middle age
- Bones become weaker and take longer to heal
- Osteoporosis may develop, in which bones become porous and easy to break
- Osteoporosis is more common in women and may result from decline in calcium and estrogen after menopause
- Deterioration of the bones under the cartilage is a condition known as osteoarthritis
- A more common form of arthritis is rheumatoid arthritis, which is a destructive disease of the joints causing pain
- During middle age, adults may begin taking anti-inflammatory medications and either steroidal or non-steroidal drugs

Reproductive Changes

- The reproductive system begins to show dramatic changes for women and less dramatic changes for men
- 73% of men and 69% of women between 40 and 49, and 67% of men and 48% of women between the ages of 50 and 59 have sex at least several times a month

Chapter Thirteen

The Climacteric and Menopause

- The loss of ability to bear children, called the climacteric, usually begins in the 40s and is complete by the late 50s
- During the climacteric, menstruation becomes irregular and eventually stops in the process of menopause
- Two processes are associated with the climacteric and menopause
  - Estrogen-related symptoms: hot flashes, night sweats, vaginal dryness, and urine leakage
  - Somatic symptoms: sleep problems, headaches, rapid heart-beat, stiffness or soreness in the joints
- African American women - more estrogen-related symptoms and less somatic symptoms
- Asian women - fewer hot flashes, more headaches, shoulder stiffness, dizziness
- Sexual activity may be affected by vaginal wall and external vaginal shrinkage and dryness. Painful intercourse and the absence of orgasm, or the need for increased stimulation for orgasm, may be experienced

Treating Symptoms of Menopause

- Decline in levels of estrogen is associated with osteoporosis, cardiovascular disease, urinary incontinence, weight gain, and memory loss
- Hormone Replacement Therapy (HRT) has been associated with both risks and benefits
  - HRT has been shown to have positive effects on the above conditions
  - HRT has been associated with increased risk of endometrial cancer and breast cancer. Lower dosages have been found to be safer, especially when combined with progestin

Reproductive Changes in Men

- A decline in sperm count of about 30%
- The prostate gland enlarges with increasing age in men and may block the urinary tract
- Testosterone gradually declines after mid-20s
- Older men report less demand to ejaculate, a need for longer stimulation to achieve erection and orgasm, and a longer phase after sex during which erection is impossible

Stress and Health

- The effect of long- and short-term stress becomes more apparent during middle-age
- Stress is highest for occupations that experience less control over their job
- Middle-aged people report higher levels of stress than older people.

Chapter Thirteen

What is Stress?

- The stress and coping paradigm is the model for which coping strategies are studied
- Stress occurs when you appraise a situation as exceeding your personal, social, or other resources and affects your well-being
- Coping is the way stress is dealt with
  - Avoiding situations, focusing on how they deal with stress, religious approaches, and sometimes by redefining the stressful situation

How are Stress and Coping Related to Physical Health?

- Chronic stress may have an effect on the immune system
- Negative events lowers the immune system, while positive events improves the immune system

Personality Types May Play a Role

- Type A behavior patterns tend to be more competitive, angry, hostile, restless, and aggressive. Type A personalities may recover from a heart attack more quickly
- Type B personalities tend to experience the opposite. Type B personalities may not be as driven to work to recover as quickly

Exercise

- Exercise slows the aging process
  - Aerobic exercise improves the functioning of the cardiovascular system
  - Studies show that middle-aged and older men that exercise moderately for 6 to 8 hours per week were less likely to die in the next week
  - Younger adults tend to exercise to improve physical appearance, while older adults are more concerned with physical and psychological health

13.2 Cognitive Development

Learning Objectives

- How does practical intelligence develop in adulthood?
- How does a person become an expert?
- What is meant by lifelong learning? What differences are there between adults and young people in how they learn?

Practical Intelligence

- Traditional methods of measuring intelligence do not reflect real-world situations
- The broad range of skills related to how individuals adapt to their physical and social environments is termed practical intelligence
- People are not as motivated to solve problems that do not have practical solutions

Denney's Theory
- The level of performance a person exhibits without practice or training is called unexercised ability
- The level of performance a normal healthy adult demonstrates under the best conditions of training is called the optimally exercised ability
- Abilities that are used and practiced more are more likely to be done accurately and quickly
- Both increase until adulthood, plateau in middle age and decline thereafter
- Research shows that practical intelligence does not appear to decline significantly until older age

Applications of Practical Intelligence
- A more practical problem is more likely to evoke an emotional response and is likely to determine the strategy for resolution
- In middle-aged adults, a practical problem is more likely to be associated with passive-dependent and avoidant-denial approaches

Becoming an Expert
- An expert is someone much better at a task than people who put little effort into it
- People develop expertise through experience, training, and practice developing strategies for accomplishing a task superior to those of non-experts
- Thinking in experts makes use of encapsulation, or connecting the thought processes to the products of thinking, making thinking more efficient

Lifelong Learning
- Occupations today rely on technology and information that change rapidly
- Learning how to learn may be a critical skill in adapting to a modern world. College educations will probably not be the last educational experience for most people
- The need for lifelong learning is clear on most college campuses in the number of middle-aged students enrolled
- Many professions require annual continuing education

13.3 Personality
Learning Objectives
- What is the five-factor model? What evidence is there for stability in personality traits?
- What changes occur in people's priorities and personal concerns? How does a person achieve generativity? How is midlife best described?

Chapter Thirteen

Stability is the Rule: The Five-Factor Model

- Costa and McCrae described personality in adulthood using five dimensions
  - Neuroticism: the extent of anxiousness, hostility, self-consciousness, impulsivity
  - Extraversion: the degree of thriving on social interaction
  - Openness to experience: a vivid imagination and dream life, appreciation of art, and desire to try anything
  - Agreeableness: being accepting, willing to work with others, and caring
  - Conscientiousness: being hard-working, ambitious, energetic, persevering

What's the Evidence for Trait Stability?

- Much research has shown that personality traits are relatively stable over 6- 12- and even 30-year spans
- This approach does not address all features of personality and may not examine those factors that are most responsive to environmental and cultural factors

Changing Priorities in Midlife

- While studies show personality traits remain stable, personal priorities change during middle-age
- Middle-aged people report desire to help young people achieve rather than their own achievement
- This desire to be productive by shaping the next generation was what Erikson called generativity
- Those who do not achieve generativity feel the effects of stagnation

What are Generative People Like?

- When inner and societal forces interconnect, a concern for the next generation becomes a priority
- Being generative helps an individual to derive meaning from their priorities and continues to shape the person's identity

Does Gender-Role Identity Converge?

- Society tends to define masculinity and femininity in traditional ways, a cross-over of gender identity in middle-age is predicted by many theories
- Research is mixed on this factor but suggests that gender identity is stable throughout young adulthood, the differences in middle-age decline
- Both men and women describe themselves as more nurturing, intimate, and tender with increasing age, though this may not show in actual behavior

Life Transition Theories and the Midlife Crisis

- Most descriptions of the stages that include a midlife crisis were based on observations of nonrepresentative groups
- Well-constructed studies indicate that a midlife crisis is not a universal experience for middle-age
- While no hard evidence exists that middle-aged adults experience a particularly tumultuous time, special challenges do exist

13.4 Family Dynamics and Middle Age

Learning Objectives

- Who are the kinkeepers in families?
- How does the relationship between middle-aged parents and their young children change?
- How do middle-aged adults deal with their aging parents?
- What styles of grandparenthood do middle-aged adults experience? How do grandchildren and grandparents interact?

Family Dynamics and Middle Age

- Women in middle-age often serve as the kinkeeper, or person who accepts the responsibility for gathering family together for celebrations and keeping them in touch
- Middle-age is often called the sandwich generation because they are often caught between caring for parents and children

Letting Go: Middle-Aged Adults & Their Children

- Becoming Friends and the Empty Nest
  - There is usually a shift in how children see their middle-aged parents. Relationships become more positive
  - Also during middle-age, parents experience the exodus of their children from the home
  - Much of the success of these transitions is predicated on the approval and encouragement parents show for their children's attempts at autonomy

When Children Come Back

- Roughly half of young adults in the U.S. move back to their parent's home at least once
- Male children, students with low GPA, low sense of autonomy, or those with an expectation that parents would provide a large portion of their income following graduation, are more likely to return to their parent's home
- Children who were abused are not as likely to return

Chapter Thirteen

Giving Back: Middle-Aged Adults and Their Aging Parents

- Caring for Aging Parents
  - Daughters are 3 times more likely to provide care than sons. Consistent across cultures
  - Parents may move in with their middle-aged children after decades of independent living, creating adjustment problems for both
  - Most adult children feel responsibility or a filial obligation to care for parents

Caregiving Stress

- Adult children may experience burnout and loss of the previous relationship
- If the caregiving situation is confining or infringes on the adult child's other obligations, the relationship may be viewed negatively and affect work, family, and self-identity
- Caregiving for parents often coincides with women's peak employment years, but research shows that employment has little effect on women's decision to provide care

Grandparenthood

- How Do Grandparents Interact with Grandchildren?
  - Grandparents may provide social and personal elements by recreational activities, passing on family histories, teaching skills, and giving advice
  - Grandchildren may help keep grandparents in touch with youth and the latest trends and technology

Being a Grandparent is Meaningful

- Some describe grandparenthood as the most important thing in their lives - centrality
- Some view grandparenthood as a time of providing wisdom and indulgence - valued elder
- Others report that interaction helps to recall the relationship they had with their own grandparents - reinvolvement with personal past
- May experience pride from knowing they will be followed by at least two generations - immortality through clan

Ethnic Differences

- Some cultures view grandparents as more burdensome, others view it as fulfilling an important role
- Native Americans may exhibit fictive grandparenting, or a practice that allows for adults to fill-in for missing or deceased grandparents
- Cultural conservator - grandchildren live with grandparents in order to learn the tribal customs

Chapter Thirteen

When Grandparents Care for Grandchildren

- In today's society, grandparents are more likely to live a farther distance from their grandchildren
- Many grandparents are the custodial parents for their grandchildren
- Lack of legal consideration of the role of grandparents has traditionally made this role more difficult, especially for obtaining records and school-related activities

Chapter Fourteen
The Personal Context of Later Life: Physical, Cognitive, and Mental Health Issues

14.1 What Are Older Adults Like?

Learning Objectives

- What are the characteristics of older adults in the population?
- How long will most people live? What factors influence this?
- What is the distinction between the third and fourth age?

The Demographics of Aging

- The population of older adults in industrialized nations has been increasing rapidly in the 20th century
- Demographers study population trends and use population pyramids to illustrate the changes
- Their research predicts that in the year 2030 the number of people over 65 will equal the number in other age groups

The Diversity of Older Adults

- Older women outnumber older men in all ethnic groups in the U.S.
- The number of older people in ethnic minority groups in the U.S. is increasing faster than in European Americans
- Currently, 50% of people over 65 have high school diplomas and 10% have college degrees. By 2030, 75% will have college degrees

Longevity

- Longevity is the number of years a person can expect to live
- Three types of longevity
  - Average life expectancy is the age at which half the people born in a particular year will have died
  - Useful life expectancy is the number of years a person is free from debilitating chronic disease
  - Maximum life expectancy is the oldest age to which any person lives

Genetic and Environmental Factors in Life Expectancy

- Heredity is a major factor in longevity
- Environment plays a role through the effects of disease and toxins
- Social class plays a role because certain conditions are related to lack of access to health care

Chapter Fourteen

Ethnic and Gender Differences in Life Expectancy

- Life expectancy is complex and varies among ethnic groups
- European American life expectancy is longer than that of African Americans', but not as long as for Hispanic Americans
- Life expectancy varies at different ages
- Women live longer than men by about 7 years. For those who live to 85, the difference is only 1 year
- Men are more susceptible to infectious diseases and other conditions that are likely to be fatal
- While many explanations have been offered, no consistent finding has been found that supports one theory

International Differences in Longevity

- Dramatic differences exist between longevity statistics among countries
  - 38 in Sierra Leone
  - 80 in Japan
- Genetic, sociocultural, and healthcare factors contribute to the differences

The Third-Fourth Age Distinction

- Third Age adults are between the ages of 60 to 80
  - Many advances in knowledge and technology have contributed to the better quality of life for this group
- Fourth Age adults are over 80
  - Few interventions have been developed to hold back cognitive and physiological declines in this group

14.2 Physical Changes and Health

Learning Objectives

- What are the major biological theories of aging?
- What physiological changes normally occur in later life?
- What are the principal health issues for older adults?

Chapter Fourteen

Biological Theories of Aging

- Wear-and-tear theory suggests that the body simply wears out
- Cellular theories focus on the buildup of toxic cellular substances and subsequent deterioration
  - Some research indicates that cells have an absolute limit on the number of times they can divide
- Other Approaches
  - Free radicals - chemicals produced by cell division that cause cell damage
  - Cross-linking is an explanation that suggests that certain proteins interact with body tissue, which results in stiffer tissues. Heart, muscle, and arteries can be affected
- Metabolic Theories
  - These theories examine the interaction between caloric intake and stress
- Programmed Cell Death Theories
  - This approach points to evidence that aging is genetically programmed
  - Recent information about human genetics is contributing to these explanations

Physiological Changes

- Changes in the Neurons
  - The fibers in the axon form spiral-shaped masses called neurofibrillary tangles, which interfere with transmission of signals
  - Damaged or defective neurons collect and form neuritic plaques, which interfere with other, healthy neurons
  - Structural and functional imaging show age-related changes in the brain associated with cognitive processes

Cardiovascular and Respiratory Systems

- Cardiovascular diseases increase dramatically with advancing age
- By young adulthood collection of fat in the arteries and in and around the heart decrease the efficiency of the circulatory system
- These changes increase the chances of cerebral vascular accidents (CVAs), which results in hemorrhage
- Older adults may experience transient ischemic attacks (TIAs), or interruptions of blood flow which can be warnings of stroke
- Older adults may have many smaller CVAs, resulting in vascular dementia
- The most common respiratory disease in older adults is chronic obstructive pulmonary disease (COPD) such as emphysema caused by smoking

Chapter Fourteen

Parkinson's Disease

- Symptoms such as slow tremors in the hands and slow walking
- Caused by deterioration of the neurons in the midbrain that use the neurotransmitter dopamine
- Victims of Parkinson's include Michael J. Fox, Muhammad Ali, Janet Reno, and Pope John Paul II
- 30-50% of people with Parkinson's develop cognitive impairments similar to those of Alzheimer's disease

Sensory Changes

- Eye and Vision Changes
  - A decrease in the amount of light admitted to the eye results in the need for increased light for reading
  - Presbyopia is the age-related decline in the ability to see close objects clearly
- Cataracts, or opaque spots in the lens of the eye, may develop. Also, glaucoma, or an increase in the pressure of the fluid in the eye, may cause loss of vision
- Retinal changes such as those caused by diabetes and macular degeneration increase in older age
- Structural changes in the eye may result in loss of visual acuity, or the ability to see detail, especially in low lighting
- Hearing loss is one of the most common normative changes in older adults
- The most common age-related hearing problem is presbycusis, which is caused by the cumulative effects of noise and age-related changes. This results in the loss of the ability to hear low-pitched sounds
- Taste, touch, temperature, and pain sensitivity do not decline as significantly in older years
- The ability to detect and distinguish smells declines after the age of 70 in many people
- Older people fall more often due to changes in the sense of balance

Health Issues

- Sleep is often problematic in older ages, disrupting the circadian rhythm, or sleep-wake cycle
- Older adults may experience nutritional deficits because of declining health and eating patterns
- The incidence of cancer increases with age and suggests the importance of screenings

Immigrant Status

- Immigrants may have language barriers that interfere with obtaining health care
- Health examinations may be affected by communication problems
- Higher rates of depression are noted among older immigrant Mexican Americans

Chapter Fourteen

14.3 Cognitive Processes

Learning Objectives

- What changes occur in information processing as people age? How do these changes relate to everyday life?
- What changes occur in memory with age? What can be done to remediate these changes?
- What is creativity and wisdom, and how do they relate to age?

Information Processing

- Older adults do more poorly on selective attention tasks
  - Vigilance, or sustained attention, may decline with age, though studies are inconsistent
  - The ability to focus, switch, and divide attention is called attentional control and may show some decline.in older age

Psychomotor Speed

- The speed at which a person can make a specific motor response may slow with advancing age
- This finding may be due to taking longer to decide what response to make, especially when faced with an ambiguous situation
- These changes make driving with advancing age a controversial issue

Working Memory

- Working memory is the information that is being used at the moment
- Working memory typically declines with age
- A combination of declining working memory and psychomotor speed may explain cognitive performance in older adults

Memory

- Explicit memory is the deliberate and conscious remembering of information
  - Episodic memory is memory of information from a specific time or event
  - Semantic memory is the remembering of the meaning of words or concepts unrelated to a specific time or event
- Implicit memory is unconscious remembering of information learned at an earlier time

What Changes?

- Episodic memory is worse in older adults than younger adults
- Older adults are not as good at spontaneously using memory strategies to improve recall
- No age differences in implicit and semantic memory have been found
- For all groups, memory is better for events that occur between ages of 10 and 30 years

Chapter Fourteen

The Impact of Beliefs About Memory Aging

- Stereotypes about older people and memory loss impacts what elderly people believe about their own abilities, affecting strategies for remembering

When Is Memory Change Abnormal?

- Most people worry about memory loss and its possible implications for disease
- When memory problems seriously affect everyday life, a serious problem may be suspected

Remediating Memory Problems

- External aids are devices and materials that rely on environmental resources such as calendars and notebooks
- Internal aids are methods that rely on mental processes such as imagery
- The E-I-E-I-O method combined these two types of help to improve memory

Creativity and Wisdom

- Creativity - the ability to produce work that is novel, in high demand, and task-appropriate
  - Creativity increases through the 20s, plateaus during the 30s, and slowly declines thereafter
  - Different disciplines and arts have varying creativity peaks
- Wisdom (Baltes and Staudinger)
  - Wisdom deals with important matters of life and the human experience
  - Wisdom is superior knowledge, judgment, and advice
  - Wisdom is knowledge with extraordinary scope, depth, and balance
  - When used, wisdom is well-intended and combines mind and virtue
  - This research showed no association between wisdom and age

What Makes One Wise?

- General personal conditions, such as mental ability
- Specific expertise conditions, such as practice or mentoring
- Facilitative life contexts, such as education or leadership experiences

14.4 Mental Health & Intervention

Learning Objectives

- How does depression in older adults differ from depression in younger adults? How is it diagnosed and treated?
- How are anxiety disorders treated in older adults?
- What is Alzheimer's disease? How is it diagnosed and managed? What causes it?

Chapter Fourteen

Depression

- Depression is diagnosed based on two changes: Feelings and physical changes
  - Feelings of sadness are called dysphoria
  - Physical changes include loss of appetite, insomnia, and trouble breathing
  - Evaluation of older adults is difficult because some of these changes may be normal

What Causes Depression?

- Biological and physical causes may include imbalances in neurotransmitters
- Internal belief systems may play a role in how people interpret things that happen to them

How Is Depression Treated in Older Adults?

- Medicines that affect the levels of neurotransmitters, such as heterocyclic antidepressants (HCAs), monamine oxidase inhibiters (MAOIs), and selective seratonin reuptake inhibitors (SSRIs), may be used
- Psychotherapy in the forms of behavior therapy or cognitive therapy may be used to learn new behaviors or examine the way patients think about their experiences

Anxiety Disorders

- Anxiety disorders include phobias and obsessive-compulsive disorder
- Anxiety disorders are more common in older adults, partly due to loss of health, relocation of residence, isolation, loss of independence, and other factors
- Anxiety disorders can often be successfully treated with psychotherapy and medications

Dementia: Alzheimer's Disease

- Dementia is a family of diseases that results in serious behavioral and cognitive impairments. Alzheimer's disease is one of the more common
- Alzheimer's disease may cause confusion, disability, and dependence
- The incidence of Alzheimer's disease increases with age. Women are at greater risk

What Are the Symptoms of Alzheimer's Disease?

- Declines in memory, attention, and judgment
- Confusion and difficulties in communication
- Changes in personality and decline in hygiene
- Incontinence, or the loss of bladder or bowel control

How Is Alzheimer's Disease Diagnosed?

- Diagnosis can only be confirmed by autopsy
- Diagnosis is made by microscopic analysis of neurons in the brain
- The diagnosis of possible Alzheimer's disease is based on extensive psychoneurological testing and ruling out other causes for symptoms

What Causes Alzheimer's Disease?

- The exact cause is not known
- Possible explanations have included a slow-acting virus and aluminum deposits in the brain. These have not be confirmed
- Genetic research has shown promising results in identifying genetic markers related to specific genes

What Can Be Done for Victims of Alzheimer's Disease?

- Though symptoms can be successfully treated, no cure exists
- Galantamine appears to help memory loss but does not reverse the deficits
- Thioridazine and haloperidol are used to treat severe psychotic symptoms
- Antidepressants may be used to treat the depression that often goes along with the disease

Chapter Fifteen
Social Aspects of Later Life: Psychosocial, Retirement, Relationship, and Societal Issues

15.1 Theories of Psychosocial Aging

Learning Objectives

- What is continuity theory?
- What is the competence and environmental press model, and how do docility and proactivity relate to the model?

Continuity Theory

- Continuity theory proposes that people use familiar strategies to cope with daily life
  - Too little continuity promotes a feeling that life is too unpredictable
  - Too much continuity promotes boredom
  - Optimal continuity allows for challenges and interest without overwhelming

Competence and Environmental Press

- Competence is the upper limit of a person's ability to function in physical health, sensory-perceptual skills, motor skills, cognitive skills, and ego strength
- Environmental press is the physical, interpersonal, or social demands of the environment
- Both factors change as we move through life and interact with life's changes
- Our adaptation level is the level at which press level is average for a particular level of competence
- Slight increases in press results in the zone of maximum performance potential, which results in increased performance
- Slight decreases in press result in the zone of maximum comfort in which people are able to live without worrying about environmental demands
- When people exert control over their lives by choosing new behaviors to meet their needs or desires, it is called proactivity
- When people allow the situation to dictate their options, they show docility
- Research shows people with high competence more often choose proactivity. Low competence results in more docility

15.2 Personality, Social Cognition & Spirituality

Learning Objectives

- What is integrity in late life? How do people achieve it?
- How is well-being defined in adulthood? How do people view themselves differently as they age?
- What role does spirituality play in late life?

Chapter Fifteen

Integrity Versus Despair

- Older people engage in life review in which they reflect often and long on the events and experiences of their lifetime
  - Some individuals judge their life to have been meaningful and productive and feel good about the choices they have made, resulting in ego integrity
  - Others feel a sense of meaninglessness and blame others for their problems, resulting in despair

Well-Being and Social Cognition

- Subjective well-being is a positive feeling about one's life
  - Subjective well-being may be based on marital status, social network, chronic illness, and stress
  - Women may experience less subjective well-being

Religiosity & Spiritual Support

- Religious faith and spirituality are important means by which older people cope with life
  - Spiritual support is involvement with organized and unorganized religious activities and pastoral care
  - Faith in God's help is described by elders as distinguishing between what can and cannot be changed, doing what one can to change the things they can, and letting go of those things that cannot be changed

15.3 I Used to Work at... Living in Retirement

Learning Objectives

- What does being retired mean?
- Why do people retire?
- How satisfied are retired people?
- How do retirees keep busy?

What Does Being Retired Mean?

- Retirement does not always mean complete withdrawal from the work environment
- Some elders have a bridge job, or a job one holds between ending their primary employment and final retirement
- Bridge jobs are associated with both retirement and overall life satisfaction

Why Do People Retire?

- Today, more people retire by choice than for any other reason
  - Most people retire when they feel they are financially secure
  - Some people retire when physical health problems interfere with work
  - People with jobs that are physically demanding tend to retire earlier

Gender Differences

- Women enter the workforce later and have more interruptions in their work history. They also may have different financial needs
- Women with husbands that have poor health or with larger numbers of dependents tend to retire earlier. The opposite is true for men

Ethnic Differences

- There are differences in what retirement means among ethnic groups, making comparisons difficult
- There are no gender differences in retirement among African Americans

Adjustment to Retirement

- Adjustment to retirement develops over time as an interplay between physical health, financial status, voluntary retirement status, and feelings of personal control
- Men who place high priority on family report more retirement satisfaction
- Women's satisfaction with retirement is not associated with any specific roles
- Research does not find the belief that health begins to decline right after retirement to have any validity

Keeping Busy in Retirement

- Organizations for retirees such as the AARP have increased the availability of activities and interests among the retired
- Retirees volunteer and find ways to provide service to others
- Volunteering supports a personal sense of purpose

15.4 Friends & Family in Late Life

Learning Objectives

- What role do friends and family play in late life?
- What are older adults' marriages like?
- What is it like to provide basic care for one's partner?
- How do people cope with widowhood? How do men and women differ?
- What special issues are involved in being a great-grandparent?

Friends and Siblings

- Friendships
  - Patterns of friendships in late life are similar to those in young adulthood
  - Older adults have fewer relationships than younger adults
  - Friendships form on the basis of many factors that are more relevant at different times, a process known as socioemotional selectivity

Chapter Fifteen

Sibling Relationships

- Five Types:
  - Intimate sibling relationships - 14%
  - Congenial sibling relationships - 30%
  - Loyal sibling relationships - 34%
  - Apathetic sibling relationships - 11%
  - Hostile sibling relationships - 11%
- Older African Americans have apathetic or hostile relationships with siblings 5 times less often than European Americans

Marriage and Gay and Lesbian Partnerships

- Older couples are more likely to be similar in mental and physical health and show fewer gender differences in sources of pleasure
- Older couples usually have developed effective ways to avoid conflict
- What research has been done has not shown differences between older gay and lesbian relationships and those of heterosexuals, in terms of quality

Caring for a Partner

- Caring for a chronically ill partner is more stressful and challenging than caring for a chronically ill parent
- Division of labor has to be readjusted
- Spouses of Alzheimer's patients report more depression and decreased marital satisfaction
- Older adults who have higher feelings of competence report few hassles in caring for partners

Widowhood

- For most people, the death of a spouse is among the most traumatic experiences they will have
- More than half of all women over 65 are widows. Only 15% of men the same age are widowers
- Friends and family may not visit or socialize as much with elders after the death of a spouse
- Men are at a higher risk of dying, themselves, soon after the death of a spouse
  - Some researchers believe that a man's wife is often his only close friend and confidant
  - There is evidence that older men are less likely to be able to carry out routine activities such as shopping and financial responsibilities
- Women are usually less financially secure when widowed and are more likely to enter poverty status
- Widowers are 5 times more likely to remarry than widows

Chapter Fifteen

Great-Grandparenthood

- For most adults, grandparenting is an enjoyable and important role
- Three important aspects of great-grandparenthood:
  - It gives a sense of personal and family renewal
  - Great-grandchildren provide new diversions and a positive new role
  - A major milestone of longevity, which is usually viewed positively

15.5 Social Issues & Aging

Learning Objectives

- Who are frail older adults? How common is frailty?
- Who are the most likely people to live in nursing homes? What are the characteristics of good nursing homes?
- How do you know whether an older adult is abused or neglected? Which people are most likely to be abused and to be abusers?
- What are the key social policy issues affecting older adults?

Frail Older Adults

- Frail older adults have physical disabilities, are very ill, or may have cognitive or psychological disorders
- A minority of older adults are frail but the percentage increases with advancing age
- Activities of Daily Living (ADLs) assess the basic daily living task competencies of older adults
- Instrumental Activities of Daily Living (IADLs) are tasks that require intellectual competence and planning

Prevalence of Frailty

- Less than 5% of adults aged 65 to 74 need assistance
- Incidence of needing assistance increases dramatically thereafter
- Older adults may also have higher rates of anxiety and depression

Living in Nursing Homes

- Only about 5% of older adults live in nursing homes
- About 50% of those who live beyond 85 will spend at least some time in a nursing home
- The increase in the number of assisted-living facilities, for older adults who need help but are not so impaired to require 24-hour care, is decreasing the number of older adults in nursing homes

Chapter Fifteen

Who Lives in Nursing Homes?

- Widowed or divorced, financially disadvantaged, without living family, very old, and European American
- Risk factors include:
  - Over age 85, Female
  - Recently admitted to a hospital
  - Lives in retirement housing
  - Unmarried or living alone
  - Has no children nearby
  - Has cognitive impairment, has problem with IADLs

What Characterizes a Good Nursing Home?

- High quality of life for residents
- Quality of care
- Safety
- Researchers suggest a "person-centered planning" approach to nursing home policies
  - This approach promotes residents' well-being by increasing their feelings of personal control
  - Nursing home staff should avoid patronizing speech and infantilization (i.e., using first names when inappropriate, terms of endearment, etc.)

Elder Abuse and Neglect

- There are several different categories of elder abuse
  - Physical
  - Sexual abuse
  - Emotional or psychological abuse
  - Financial or material exploitation
  - Abandonment
  - Neglect
  - Self-neglect

Prevalence

- Estimates are that there were 551,000 people over the age of 60 abused or neglected in the U.S. in 1996
- The most common types of abuse were:
  - Neglect - 60%
  - Physical abuse - 16%
  - Financial or material exploitation - 12%

Characteristics of Elder Abuse Victims

- People over the age of 80 are 2 to 3 times more likely to be abused than those under age 80
- In 90% of the cases where the perpetrator of elder abuse is known, it was a family member, 2/3 of which were a spouse or adult child
- Recently, telemarketing fraud has become a larger problem

Chapter Fifteen

Causes of Elder Abuse

- Research fails to support the theories that stress alone, or that patterns of abuse transmitted across generations, causes abuse
- Abuse is more likely to be caused by a combination of:
  - Intrapersonal problems of the caregiver
  - Interpersonal problems of the caregiver
  - Social characteristics of the care recipient

Politics, Social Security, and Medicare

- As the number of older adults has increased, so has the quality of their everyday lives, partly as a result of increasing political power
- In the 1950s, roughly 35% of older adults were below the poverty line compared to about 11% in the mid-1990s

The Political Landscape

- The cost of Medicare, Social Security, and other federal programs began to be larger proportions of the federal budget as the numbers of elders increased in the 1970s
- Elders began to be the scapegoats of budgetary problems, resulting in program reform
- Political pressure increased to ensure that programs treated all generations fairly

Political Activity

- Adults over the age of 65 are the most politically active of all groups
- While only representing 16% of all registered voters, they constituted 20% of all voters in the 1996 presidential election
- The AARP is the largest interest group in the U.S. and has political power and influence

Social Security

- Created in 1935 by Franklin Roosevelt to protect the average American and his family against the possibility of poverty in old age
- Social Security has become the primary source of financial support after retirement for most U.S. citizens
- Baby boomers will be followed by a smaller generation that will not generate payroll taxes sufficient to pay for it

Medicare

- 40 million U.S. citizens depend on Medicare for medical insurance
- To be eligible, a person must be over 65, be disabled, or have permanent kidney failure
- Part A covers inpatient hospital services
- Part B covers the cost of physicians, outpatient services, medical equipment, and other health supplies
- Medicare includes prescription assistance

Chapter Sixteen
The Final Passage: Dying and Bereavement

16.1 Definitions & Ethical Issues

Learning Objectives

- How is death defined?
- What legal and medical criteria are used to determine when death occurs?
- What are the ethical dilemmas surrounding euthanasia?

Sociocultural Definitions of Death

- Different cultures view death in diverse ways
- Customs and expectations also differ in rituals of bereavement and mourning
- Even within a culture there is diversity in the view of death, mourning, and bereavement

There Are at Least 10 Ways Death Can Be Viewed

- Death as an image or object
- Death as a statistic
- Death as an event
- Death as a boundary
- Death as a state of being

Legal and Medical Definitions

- The traditional definition of clinical death was a lack of heartbeat and respiration
- Today, brain death is the most used definition:
  - No spontaneous movement to stimulation
  - No spontaneous respiration for 1 hour
  - Lack of response to pain
  - No eye movements, blinking, or pupil responses
  - No postural activity, swallowing, or yawning
  - No motor reflexes
  - A flat EEG for 10 minutes
  - No change in any of these in 24 hours
- All eight criteria must be met and other possible conditions ruled out
- In most hospitals, the lack of brain activity must extend to the brainstem and cortex
- Activity only in the brainstem is called a persistent vegetative state, from which the person does not recover

Ethical Issues

- Bioethics is the study of the combination of human values and technological advances
  - Bioethics grew from the increasing concern for respect for individual freedom and the difficult task of defining morality in medical care

Euthanasia

- Euthanasia is the practice of ending life for reasons of mercy
  - Extends from the advances that allow for life to be extended by extraordinary means, and the concern for quality of life and respect for the individual

Active Euthanasia

- Active euthanasia is the deliberate ending of someone's life
- Moral and religious concerns are involved in the issue of active euthanasia
- Physician-assisted suicide has become an increasingly controversial issue
- Some states have passed laws specifically making physician-assisted suicide legal, others have banned it

Passive Euthanasia

- Allowing a person to die by withholding available treatment is called passive euthanasia
- A survey in England showed that caregivers agreed that dementia patients should not receive treatments when critically ill
- Most cases of passive euthanasia end up in court which has asserted that without advance directives, nourishment cannot be stopped

Making Your Intentions Known

- There are two ways to tell others of your choice about final decisions
  - A living will in which a person states their preferences and intentions in the event that they may be unable to make their intentions known
  - A durable power of attorney names an individual who will have the legal authority to make decisions and speak for the person

16.2 Thinking About Death: Personal Aspects

Learning Objectives

- How do feelings about death change over adulthood?
- How do people deal with their own death?
- What is death anxiety, and how do people show it?
- How do people deal with end-of-life issues and create a final scenario?
- What is hospice?

Chapter Sixteen

A Life Course Approach to Dying

- Young adults integrate feeling and emotions with their thinking about death, lessening their feelings of immortality
- Middle-age adults think about their own death as they deal with the death of their parents
- Older adults are less anxious about death because of achievement of ego integrity and because of declining joy of living
- Dealing With One's Own Death
- Reactions to impending death can vary in its development, especially with different causes of terminal illness
  - Diseases such as cancer may have a terminal phase in which a patient may be able to predict and prepare for death
  - Some diseases that do not have a terminal phase may create a condition in which a person's death could occur at any time

Kubler-Ross' Theory

- Elisabeth Kubler-Ross began working with terminally ill patients
- During this time, terminally ill patients were not always told they were dying, and death was not generally a topic of discussion. Her research was controversial
- Kubler-Ross began to study patients' reactions to their terminal illness and found that most people experienced certain emotional states

Kubler-Ross' Stages of Dying

- Denial - Shock and disbelief
- Anger - Hostility and resentment
- Bargaining - Looking for a way out
- Depression - No longer able to deny, patients experience sadness and loss
- Acceptance - Acceptance of the inevitability of death with peace and detachment
- Though not all people experience all stages in the same order, discussion of death helps to move toward acceptance

A Contextual Theory of Dying

- Stage theories imply order to the transition toward acceptance that may not exist
- Stage theories do not state what moves a person through the stages
- Observations suggest that people vary greatly in the duration of a particular stage
- There is no single correct way to die
- Each person's own view of their death and need for health care may impact their movement through the stages

Chapter Sixteen

Death Anxiety

- Terror management theory asserts that the continuation of one's life is the primary motive behind all behavior. Fear of dying is consistent with this motive
- Research suggests that death anxiety includes pain, body malfunction, humiliation, rejection, etc. Each of these factors can be assessed in any of three levels: public, private, and unconscious
- Death anxiety may be lower in older adults due to ego integrity and a positive life review. Emotional problems are predictive of higher death anxiety

Learning to Deal With Death Anxiety

- Adolescents engage in more risk-taking behavior which suggests less death anxiety
- Reduction can be achieved by contemplating one's own death by writing one's own obituary, planning one's own funeral, etc.
- Death education strives to address death anxiety by presenting factual information about death and reducing sensitivity to the issues involved

Creating a Final Scenario

- Discussions of the issues of management of the final phase of life and the after-death disposition of their body are called end-of-life issues
- Hospitals and nursing homes teach about advance directives like durable power of attorney and living wills
- Making one's choices known and providing information about how one wants their life to end is called a final scenario

Chapter Sixteen

The Hospice Option

- An alternative to going to a hospital or nursing home during a terminal illness is hospice care. This involves assisting dying people with pain management and a death with dignity
- The emphasis of hospice is on quality of life
- The primary goal of hospice is to make the person comfortable and peaceful, not to delay an inevitable death
- St. Christopher's Hospice in England was founded by Dr. Cicely Saunders and is the model for modern hospices
- When no treatment or cure is possible, hospice care is requested. The family and the patient is viewed as a unit
- May be inpatient or outpatient
- An emphasis is placed on patient dignity
- Patients show less anxiety and depression
- Key questions about the possible use of hospice services:
    - Does the person know the truth about their condition?
    - What options are available for patient care?
    - What are the patient's expectations?
    - How well do the people in the person's social network communicate?
    - Are family members available to provide care?
    - Is a high-quality hospice care program available?

16.3 Surviving the Loss: The Grieving Process

Learning Objectives

- How do people experience the grief process?
- What feelings do grieving people have?
- What is the difference between normal and abnormal grief?

The Grieving Process

- Bereavement is the state or condition caused by loss through death
- Grief is the sorrow, hurt, anger, guilt, confusion, and other feelings that arise after suffering a loss
- Mourning is the way in which we express our grief
- Mourning rituals can be fairly standard across a culture. Grief varies greatly

Chapter Sixteen

The Grief Process

- People must do several things during grief
    - Acknowledge the realty of the loss
    - Work through the emotional turmoil
    - Adjust to the environment where the deceased is absent
    - Loosen the ties to the deceased
- It is important to remember that grief is a process. We must avoid several mistakes
    - No two people grieve exactly the same
    - We must not underestimate the length of time people need to deal with the various issues. One year is needed and 2 years may be required

Risk Factors in Grief

- Mode of death affects the grief process. When death is anticipated, people experience anticipatory grief that allows for working through some of the issues ahead of time
- The strength of attachment to the deceased makes a difference in the amount of time and difficulty of the grief process
- Two risk factors have been researched: lack of social support and kinship

Normal Grief Reactions

- Coming to terms with bereavement is called grief work
- Grief work consists of coping, affect, change, and relationship
- Many people experience anniversary reactions, which are changes in behavior related to feelings of sadness on the date of the loss

Grief Over Time

- Rosenblatt reports that people still feel the effects of the deaths of family members 50 years after the event
- The length of time did not diminish the depth of the emotions experienced
- Religiosity has been investigated as a source of support for people following the loss of a loved one. The results are mixed as to whether this factor provides help

Coping With Grief

- Two processes have been proposed to explain grief
    - The four component model lists:
- The context of the loss
- The continuation of subjective meaning associated with loss
- The changing representations of the loss relationship over time
- The role of coping and emotion-regulation processes

Chapter Sixteen

The Dual Process Model of coping with bereavement (DPM)

- Lists two types of stressors
  - Loss-oriented stressors - those having to do with the loss itself
  - Restoration-oriented stressors - those related to adapting to the survivor's new life situation

Traumatic Grief Reactions

- Traumatic grief involves
  - Symptoms of separation distress - preoccupation with the deceased to the point that it interferes with everyday functions
  - Symptoms of traumatic distress - mistrust, anger, and detachment from others

16.4 Dying and Bereavement Experiences Across the Life Span

Learning Objectives

- What do children understand about death? How should adults help them deal with it?
- How do adolescents deal with death?
- How do adults deal with death? What are the special issues they face concerning the death of a child or parent?
- How do older adults face the loss of a child, grandchild, or partner?

Childhood

- Areas of developmental change affecting a child's understanding of death and grief
  - Cognitive-language ability
  - Psychosocial development
  - Coping skills
- Children's coping methods may include:
  - Regression
  - Guilt for causing the death
  - Denial
  - Displacement
- Bereavement in childhood usually does not have long-lasting effects such as depression, if the child gets adequate care
- A child may have difficulty with the concept of death if adults are not open and honest with them
  - The use of euphemisms such as "gone away," or "only sleeping," can confuse and cause literal interpretation

Adolescence

- 50% of college students have experienced the loss of a family member or friend in the past two years
- Young adolescents are reluctant to express or discuss their grief and they may be more likely to experience psychosomatic symptoms
- Adolescents who lose a parent may show many similar behaviors to those who have lost a sibling

Chapter Sixteen

Adulthood

- Young adults may feel that those who die at this point are cheated out of their future
- Loss of a partner in young adulthood is very difficult because the loss is so unexpected
- Losing a spouse in middle adulthood results in challenging basic assumptions about self, relationships, and life options
- Loss in middle adulthood may result in shifting of thinking of how long they have lived to how much time they have left

Death of One's Child in Young and Middle Adulthood

- Mourning is intense and some never reconcile the loss
- Young parents who lose a child to SIDS report high anxiety, more negative view of the world, and guilt
- A parent's attachment to a child begins before the birth and loss of a child during childbirth can be very traumatic
  - People are expected by society to recover quickly from such an experience

Death of One's Parent

- When a parent dies, the loss hurts but also causes the loss of a buffer between ourselves and death. We may feel that we are now next in line
- Death of a parent may result in a loss of a source of guidance, support, and advice
- The loss of a parent may result in complex emotions including relief, guilt, and a feeling of freedom

Late Adulthood

- Older adults are often less anxious about death and more accepting of it
- Elders may feel that their most important life tasks have been completed
- Older adults are more likely to have experienced loss before

Death of One's Child or Grandchild in Late Life

- Older bereaved parents may have guilt that the pain of a loss of a child affected the relationships with surviving children
- Many grieving parents report that the relationship with the deceased child was the closest they ever had
- Bereaved grandparents tend to hide their grief behavior in an attempt to shield the grieving parents from the level of grief being felt

Death of One's Partner

- Society expects the surviving spouse to mourn for a period of time. Different cultures have varying "acceptable" lengths of time expectations
- The support system for the bereaved spouse is very important in determining the duration and outcome of grief
- Loss of a spouse leaves a positive bias for the memory of the relationship with the deceased